Fourth Ward Charlotte

A NEIGHBORHOOD HISTORY

Cameron Holtz

Published by The History Press
Charleston, SC
www.historypress.com

First published 2023

Manufactured in the United States

ISBN 9781467154260

Library of Congress Control Number: 2023945811

For Dennis Rash.

Dennis loved the Fourth Ward and was a passionate promoter of the community he helped create here. His intellect and work ethic were matched with a boundless curiosity. His generous and thoughtful spirit made him a wonderful neighbor. His gift for storytelling inspired so many others to share their own stories, and we are so lucky to have had his friendship.

CONTENTS

ACKNOWLEDGEMENTS

All quotes are taken from interviews recorded between 2016 and 2023. They have been lightly edited for clarity.

I deeply appreciate the people who sat with me for interviews and shared their memories. These stories are why I wanted to write this book and honor the work that went into creating our wonderful neighborhood.

Thanks to Robin Cochran for giving me the initial challenge to collect these stories and for all of the ways she has shaped Fourth Ward and the Charlotte arts landscape.

Thanks to Betty Chafin Rash for entrusting me with Dennis's voluminous slide collection documenting the Ninth Street house move and general Uptown development. These have been digitized and will be housed at the J. Murrey Atkins Library at UNC Charlotte.

While the photos included here are from numerous sources, my special thanks to Jim Renegar and Gloria Coltharp. They took and kept many of the personal photographs of Fourth Ward "in progress," and I am deeply grateful to them for sharing this documentation.

Catherine Barnhardt Browning generously gave me the scrapbooks she kept for decades with details of the Berryhill House renovation, Berryhill Foundation moves and sales and her personal memorabilia. They were instrumental in beginning this work and prompted many fond memories from interviewees.

The modern photos of the houses were taken by Austin Caine and are shared with his permission. Austin's appreciation for these places and his dedication for capturing their spirit shines through the images.

PREFACE

My connection to these stories began in 2000, when my husband and I moved to Charlotte. We explored several neighborhoods, but as soon as we found Fourth Ward, we knew we wanted to make our home here. Luckily, one of the original Victorians was up for sale and we were able to buy it—our first and forever house.

To learn more about our new city, I began to volunteer with the neighborhood group, Friends of Fourth Ward, and with Historic Charlotte, a preservation nonprofit affiliate of the local Landmarks Commission. Years later, as some of the folks who had founded the modern Fourth Ward were aging or moving away, I realized the importance of recording their stories before they were lost altogether. Many of these "urban homesteaders" had boxes of slides and photos, clippings and meeting minutes that they shared, and that became the basis for much of this book. They also shared their stories in hours of interviews, with a lot of laughing and a few tears along the way.

As I worked to match photos and stories to the houses as they are today, one presented a major challenge. The details on the building are clearly visible and several of the original homeowners remember it being moved, but it didn't match any of the known moved houses in the neighborhood. For several weeks, I walked around with a copy of the photo in hand, checking the back face of one building, the hidden side of another, trying to figure out where the house had landed.

Success finally came one afternoon after leaves had fallen in the late fall. As I drove down the ramp from Highway 277, I could see the long-sought roofline with its distinctive dentil molding! The house had been moved to 326 West Tenth Street, a bit out of the core residential area, and had been turned into a lawyer's office. Hidden behind beautiful mature trees and without a resident to identify her, the house had been almost unnoticed, just around the corner.

To me, that's emblematic of the beauty of Fourth Ward. It's a lovely little gem, tucked into the corner of bustling Charlotte's Uptown, quietly persevering.

Introduction

FROM FLOURISHING TO DERELICT AND BACK AGAIN

Walk through Fourth Ward today and you will see a charming neighborhood of lovingly maintained Victorian homes mixed with smart brick townhouses and a sprinkle of modern homes. The brick sidewalks and tree-lined streets are pedestrian friendly. Traffic is tamed with frequent cul-de-sacs, one-way streets and stop signs. A large park anchors the heart of the neighborhood, and small green spaces pop up in many places to further calm both traffic and the soundscape.

The people you encounter will likely be a mixture, too: professionals walking between work and home; parents with laden strollers; older kids waiting for the bus; joggers in the early morning and evenings; elderly neighbors just back from the grocery store down the street.

It is easy, today, to understand that Fourth Ward was the most sought-after address when many of those Victorians were built. From the 1880s to the 1920s, it was the home of Charlotte's elite—businessmen, elected officials, church leaders, professionals. Their families attended the neighborhood's churches and schools; their wives led the city's social life from grand porches and parlors.

But it is nigh impossible to imagine how different the neighborhood would have appeared at its worst, in about 1973.

The changes that began during the Depression and accelerated in the World War II era inflicted deep damage to Charlotte's urban core. Real estate developers created "streetcar suburbs" accessible by new trolley lines, and these became the new fashionable residential areas. Increasing love of and eventual dependence on cars fueled additional suburbanization. The city center was hollowed out by federally funded urban renewal projects; the Brooklyn neighborhood of Second Ward, a once-prosperous African American community, was razed and erased in the 1960s to make way for the city and county government offices. First Ward was dominated by a public housing project and Third Ward by light industry. Fourth Ward went into a long slide to poverty and neglect. While the neighborhood retained traces of its residential character, it was scarred by neglect.

Walking through the neighborhood in 1973 would have been discouraged on many counts. Heavy trucks barreled through the narrow streets, making their way from the highway to the business district. The blocks were a mix of empty lots and once-grand houses. Homes had been converted to apartments and then further divided into single-room rental houses. Eventually, many were used for prostitution or simply abandoned. Several houses were lost to fires lit by vagrants trying to keep warm. Numerous buildings were razed by the city because they had become so derelict as to constitute a public nuisance.

The most successful businesses were the "houses of ill repute" on Pine Street. The neighborhood was known for drugs, street crime and prostitution; it was considered risky during daylight hours and frankly dangerous at night.

Fourth Ward was a problem, but a few visionaries realized that it was also an opportunity. Preservationists wanted to protect the handful of remaining Victorian houses. Business leaders, especially bankers, wanted to have a better quality of life in the city center and business district. Elected officials wanted less crime and a better tax base. Civic volunteers wanted a transformative, community-scale project. This coalition found common cause in the recovery, preservation and re-creation of Fourth Ward.

As hard as it is to imagine how far Fourth Ward fell, it is inspiring to witness how it was raised back up, figuratively and literally. While each of these disparate groups and individuals was vital, none of them could have done the work alone. Exploring the ways that their efforts complemented each other is an object lesson in how to create true community.

THE SPARK OF INTEREST IN FOURTH WARD

In 1974, a grassroots group calling itself Citizens for Preservation came together in response to the demolition of the First National Bank building on South Tryon Street. To create interest in the remaining historic assets of the city, they began to document the existing older buildings in the Charlotte region. They compiled the best of the examples in a charming brochure titled *Stained Glass and Gingerbread* that showed the number of historic assets that still existed in the area. The collected photographs and short descriptive notes are often the only records of the physical state of these buildings at the time, which must be considered a low point for the area. While individual house restorations were often well documented, those records provide details for only that particular site. The full sense of the decline and possibility for renewal of the neighborhood and the individual houses is uniquely well represented in this brochure.

Up the road at UNC Charlotte, the history department had two new professors, Ed Perzel and Dan Morrill, who saw that brochure and used it to raise some academic interest in local history. They also started a sideline business in making presentations to local civic groups about the history of the area, including the garden clubs, rotary clubs and church groups.

> *I got interested in the local history that hadn't been considered very important. There were wonderful sites out near the university, like McIntyre Farm, to talk about, and I started working with the Citizens for Preservation folks. I think that they saw I was eager to work and willing to write or talk to about anybody, so I was elected president.*
>
> —*Ed Perzel*

Stained Glass and Gingerbread cover. *Courtesy of Ed Perzel.*

The women of the Junior League were looking for a meaningful public improvement project with connection to both the upcoming national bicentennial and the social justice needs of the city. Several of them heard the *Stained Glass and Gingerbread* presentation and shared their interest with the League's Environmental Committee. They were seeking a project with some heft—bigger than their usual annual efforts and tied to the upcoming national bicentennial. Committees had considered options from educational seminars to the development of a nature museum and petting zoo to a historic preservation project.

> *Patsy Kinsey came with a great talk and told us that we just had to get involved and save some of these houses in Fourth Ward. That got the ball rolling.*
>
> —*Catherine Barnhardt Browning, president of the Junior League of Charlotte*

The Berryhill House, located at 324 West Ninth Street, drew the attention of each of these groups. It was built in 1897 by a family that owned a construction business, and the ornate gingerbread, columns and complicated slate roof remained a testament to their skill. However, the interior had been carved up into multiple single-room apartments, and the house had not been maintained. It was sadly reflective of the overall condition in Fourth Ward.

The city council and staff were also looking at Fourth Ward. They wanted to address the problem of a central neighborhood with low property values and high crime rates. City Manager David Burkhalter was intimately familiar with the problems, both as a civil servant and as a member of First Presbyterian Church, which anchors the block of Trade Street between Church and Poplar Streets.

Burkhalter wanted to improve the neighborhood for the church and recognized that the land itself could have remarkable value. But there wasn't a clear protocol for how the church might address the problem. With a congregation including many lawyers and real estate professionals, he recognized that there were resources at hand to work on the problem.

He convened a group of church members to discuss how to improve the neighborhood around the church.

> *Loy McKeithen and I were charged to come up with a provocative program about it. David told me that we ought to be interested in what the Nixon administration was doing with regard to urban renewal and tax credits.*
>
> —*Dennis Rash*

Dennis Rash proved to be a linchpin for all the efforts to revitalize Fourth Ward. He had worked closely with North Carolina National Bank (NCNB, now Bank of America) as a real estate attorney; he had left the law practice to become dean of students at UNCC; and his wife at the time, Marsha, was president-elect of the Junior League.

> *So, I talked with David and Marsha and Catherine, and there were lots of ideas.…I said, "I'm pretty sure that we can't figure it out at this one session. How about if I buy chicken box lunches for everybody, and we'll get together at the* [First Presbyterian] *Fellowship Hall?"*
>
> *And that was really how I started working on Fourth Ward—all due to the fact that I was willing to buy the fried chicken and get the hall.*
>
> —*Dennis Rash*

At NCNB, Hugh McColl was a rising talent with big aspirations for the bank. He was dedicated to growing the bank's breadth and stature and just hated having the center of its home city be so boring. Building a great bank would require a much more vibrant city to attract and keep top talent.

> *There just wasn't anything there! It wasn't gentrification because the whole area was empty. Houses had burned down; some had been torn down by the city because they were so dilapidated. When I looked out at that corner of the city from our offices, it was green.*
>
> —*Hugh McColl*

A JEWEL IN THE ROUGH NEIGHBORHOOD

Renovating the Berryhill House

The serendipitous opportunity for many of these interested parties to come together came when the Junior League learned of a house for sale in the Fourth Ward, the Berryhill House. Here was an 1884 Victorian with most of the original structure and decoration intact, on a large corner lot, only blocks from the center of town. It wasn't lost on them that it was also in derelict condition and had been used as a rooming house for decades. They knew that the surrounding neighborhood was largely empty lots or similarly rundown structures, mostly as single-room occupancy operations or houses of prostitution.

The League had long been active in community programs, typically partnering with another organization for a multiyear commitment. They were instrumental in establishing the Nature Museum, Girl Scout Camp Occoneechee, Speech and Hearing Center and programs in the public schools and hospitals. For the most part, they raised money with a charity shop, an annual gala and donation drives.

The preservation of the Berryhill House was the first time that the group took on a major project without a partner. It was a big step, but the chance to have a meaningful impact in such a needy part of the community was tantalizing.

As Junior League president, Catherine Barnhardt Browning led the search for financial support for the project.

> *The Berryhill House was available for sale. Adelaide* [Davis] *and I went to Hugh McColl, and at the time he was the treasurer of the bicentennial*

Catherine Barnhardt Browning in front of a West Ninth Street apartment building. *Courtesy of Catherine Barnhardt Browning.*

> *for Charlotte. We convinced him that we needed some money to buy this house in Fourth Ward.*
>
> *Hugh talked with Rolfe Neill* [of the *Charlotte Observer*], *and the Knight Foundation put some money in and the Ivey's department store did, too.*
>
> —*Catherine Barnhardt Browning*

Hugh McColl was vice chairman at NCNB, responsible for national and international banking operations and relationships with other banks. He had become interested in efforts to revitalize the center city and saw the work of the Junior League as an indication that the neighborhood might attract a different sort of resident. The Junior League women were all middle or upper class, and many were members of "old Charlotte" families. Their engagement in the Fourth Ward would bring wider attention and broader community support. The small investment in their project would have a great impact.

McColl, too, recalled the initial meeting with the Junior League regarding the project.

> *Catherine Barnhardt came and asked for the money to save the Berryhill House. It interested me, so I gave her $25,000, and I got George Ivey to*

> *give some money. And that was really remarkable, but George was always a sucker for a pretty girl, and Catherine was quite a looker!*
>
> *—Hugh McColl*

The effort of the League to purchase the Berryhill House wasn't without controversy. The opposition largely centered on the possibility of failure and the improbability of a group of "ladies who lunch" being successful in a real estate venture.

> *My father said to me, "Catherine, women do not have that kind of analytical mind to manage money."*
>
> *It's funny now that I came from such a traditional background, and of course, my parents thought I was nuts, going to such a neighborhood where all those winos were. They said, "You're gonna get killed and raped and everything else that can go wrong!"*
>
> *—Catherine Barnhardt Browning*

Warnings came, too, from real estate professionals in Charlotte. They were certain that Fourth Ward was a lost cause, and they doubted the women's ability to execute such a complicated project in any location.

> *Henry Faison came to my living room the night before the vote and said, "If you go ahead with this, you will never get any more money from me or from…" He named several other moneyed people in Charlotte. We bought the Berryhill anyway.*
>
> *There was a good bit of opposition from the floor that night, including Molly Faison. That was hard.*
>
> *Years, many years, later he (Henry) had the good grace to pull me aside at a cocktail party and tell me that he had been wrong about that whole deal.*
>
> *—Catherine Barnhardt Browning*

The Junior League bought the Berryhill House for $40,000 on October 28, 1975.

Robin Cochran was the chair of the Junior League committee managing the Berryhill House. Her energy and dedication convinced the other volunteers of their ability to transform the wreck of a house into a showpiece again. The house looks so much better with a fresh coat of paint and the repaired porch railing, though several windows are still boarded up and awaiting replacement. *Courtesy of Catherine Barnhardt Browning.*

The Junior League's plan for the Berryhill House was simple: work on the house for six months, clean it up, ensure its preservation and sell it as a single-family home. Robin Cochran was elected to lead the Berryhill House Project Committee. As a member of an "old Charlotte" family, she was familiar with Uptown and was a true believer in its potential.

> *We had a good group, and it was such an interesting place and wasn't just a combat zone. But these girls had never been across the street from three active whorehouses!*
>
> *The important thing was to keep at it, to go every day so that we could keep some progress going. It was a lot of work, but we just kept at it.*
>
> —*Robin Cochran*

Many of the volunteers had not been to Uptown since the Belk department store closed in the late 1960s. At first, they only worked in large teams so that there were always lots of people around. Still, just being in the area could be a challenge:

Robin called me up and said, "Get your bag, we're going downtown to look at this house! We are going to get this done."

So we pull up and we're starting to poke around, and Berryhill at this point was in a total state of disrepair—the weeds were knee high and everything around it was just the slums. We are standing on the front walk, and all of a sudden, these police cars come screaming up to the house across the street, and there's all this shouting. They bring people out of that house, put them over the hood of the car and frisk them, and they're all in handcuffs.... Then they put them in the police cars and, whoosh, drive off.

This young policeman was sitting across at that house, writing it all up, and he keeps looking over at us, two little Junior League ladies in their Lilly Pulitzer dresses! Finally, he walked over and asked "Ladies, what *are you doing here?"*

Robin launches into her pitch: "Do you see this beautiful house? You have no idea how great this is all going to be. We're going to do a renovation, and it's just going to be wonderful and this whole area is going to change!"

The Berryhill House was renovated by the Junior League with support from donors such as Sears, which provided the paint, and the local banks. Volunteers stripped paint from the mantels, newel posts and stair rails. The porch supports were so rotted that they had to be completely removed and replaced, but the columns were made of a sturdier wood and were untouched by rot. *Courtesy of Dennis Rash.*

Left: Even in the midst of its rehabilitation, the details of the Berryhill House testify to the skill and artistry of the builders. The old house had suffered from neglect, but most of the work that the Junior League did was cleaning and removing old paint and wallpaper. The electrical and plumbing systems needed updating, but the structure itself was sturdy. *Courtesy of Catherine Barnhardt Browning.*

Right: A curious cat inspects the Berryhill House porch as it is torn up to be replaced. *Courtesy of Dennis Rash.*

> *The cop looked at me and said, "Is she crazy?" and I said, "Yeah, but I'm rolling with it!"*
>
> *From then and there, there was a tremendous energy around the project, and I loved being part of it.*
>
> – *Nancy Betty*

In the six months between taking ownership and opening the house to prospective buyers, the League hired contractors to address old plumbing and wiring while volunteers tackled the extensive cosmetic renovations needed.

First, there was the straightforward but very dirty work of cleaning out the detritus left by previous tenants. The house had been split up into eight different living areas, and some of the former occupants were described as "not too hygienic" in their habits. There were piles of abandoned clothing, empty bottles galore, stained mattresses and broken or worn-out furniture.

Junior League volunteers at the Berryhill House didn't just get their hands dirty. Marsha Rash Sherry recalled having so much dust in her hair and dirt under her nails that it would take two showers to really feel clean after a shift working at the house. *Courtesy of Dennis Rash.*

The interior of the Berryhill House in rough shape. *Courtesy of Dennis Rash.*

Junior League volunteers ran a farmers' market inside stripped Berryhill House to bring more people to see their work in progress. *Courtesy of Dennis Rash.*

After the clean-out, a team of volunteers stripped tattered wallpaper from almost every room, and others removed multiple layers of paint from the tiny grooves in the stair railing and the ornate mantels. The surrounding garden was overgrown with weeds and was completely cleared and replanted.

Over the six months, almost one hundred volunteers spent thousands of hours doing the hard, physical work of cleaning and restoring the Berryhill House.

> *I learned that I had a very mistaken impression of the Junior League. I thought that they were a white glove organization, and really they were a work glove organization.*
>
> —*Rolfe Neill*

The Berryhill House was formally opened to the public on May 15, 1976. Although the weather was dreary with torrential rains, the turnout was spectacular. That weekend, almost two thousand visitors came to view the completed project, and more than three hundred came each subsequent Sunday when the League opened the house for tours.*

On October 14, 1976, the Berryhill House was sold to Jim and Eileen Hester.

* Berryhill Preservation Incorporated pamphlet produced by the Junior League of Charlotte, September 1, 1976. The organization was often referred to as the Berryhill Preservation Foundation.

CIRCLING THE WAGONS

With the funds from the sale of the Berryhill House, the Junior League created a new organization to continue working on preserving houses: the Berryhill Foundation. Catherine Barnhardt Browning became its president, and many of the Junior League volunteers and former members of the Citizens for Preservation joined the effort. They quickly learned that the inventory of old homes in good enough shape for preservation was pretty small, but there were many empty lots in Fourth Ward and many houses in the Greater Charlotte area that were in danger of being torn down. Moving houses that were slated for demolition into the empty spaces seemed a natural fit. They decided to pursue dual strategies in hopes of bringing a critical mass of homes together: buy what they could preserve in the Fourth Ward, and move endangered houses into the neighboring lots.

Being that young, we could move mountains! Houses seemed pretty easy!
—Catherine Barnhardt Browning

The Berryhill Foundation also bought and stabilized one of the oldest houses in the neighborhood, at 314 West Eighth Street. While it is now recognized as a landmark, its condition at the time did not inspire much respect. It was almost smothered by overgrown shrubs and, except for the Overcarsh House two lots away, surrounded by empty lots. An article in the *Charlotte Observer* and some simple photos were the entire marketing kit for the house. Luckily, Christopher and Pam Geiger read the article and purchased the house in 1977 for $13,000.

Across the street, the new Salvation Army housing was being built. The other nearby lots were soon filled with new construction or moved homes as Fourth Ward regained popularity and new owners sought to join the neighborhood.

Catherine Barnhardt Browning became a real estate agent and represented the Berryhill Foundation in many of its sales.

Berryhill also sold the sad-looking house at 327 West Ninth, the corner of Pine and Ninth Streets, just across from the Berryhill House. As with many of the remaining structures in the neighborhood, this one had been divided into several rental units, all sharing the bathroom and kitchen.

The Berryhill Foundation worked in close collaboration with Crouch Brothers Moving Company to execute the moves. Once a viable structure and empty lot were matched, they had to coordinate with traffic authorities, the power company and other neighboring businesses.

The process of moving houses is slow and exacting. Houses with wooden frame construction are good candidates because they are comparatively light and have a centralized mass. The process involves placing steel girders beneath the structure and using jacks to lift the building off the foundation. The girders are then slid onto a flatbed truck (or two), and the whole house can then be moved to the new site. Once there, the process is reversed, setting the old house on a new foundation. The moves also necessitate the removal of any overhead power lines or other overhanging barriers between the sites, such as streetlights.

> *Crouch Brothers were the movers. Emery was the guy I worked with so much—great guy. Crouch would do all the work to figure it out: the route and which lines to take down. One house they had to cut in half! During one move, the axle broke on the truck; what a night that was. The road* [Ninth Street] *has a little dip in it. You wouldn't even notice it, except that the weight going across the axle was too much when it hit that section. The house was sitting there in the middle of the street in the middle of the night!*
>
> *They ended up calling a truck repair team that came down and replaced the axle on the truck with the house still sitting on the truck bed.*
>
> *—Catherine Barnhardt Browning*

Often, the moves took place overnight to avoid disrupting traffic, but they also attracted much attention and were well chronicled in the local media.

Right: The original two rooms of this house at 314 West Eighth Street is believed to be the oldest "residence" in Fourth Ward. *Courtesy of Catherine Barnhardt Browning.*

Below: This sales flier shows several properties that were available and the low prices they were asking. *Courtesy of Jim Renegar and Gloria Coltharp.*

What's For Sale

Are you interested in buying a house in Fourth Ward? Here is what's available and the asking price for some of the houses. (Lot sizes are in feet). For further information on these houses or other property in Fourth Ward, contact Catherine Barnhardt at Berryhill Preservation Inc., 372-7419, weekdays between 9 a.m. and 5 p.m., or a real estate agent.

Kenmore Hotel
229 N. Poplar St.

424 N. Poplar St.
$10,000
2,400 sq. ft.
Lot 52 x 99.5

712 N. Pine St.
$18,000
2,540 sq. ft
Lot 38 x 118

Berryhill Store Complex
$50,000

1109 S. Caldwell St.
$3,000
1,400 sq. ft.
Must be moved to Fourth Ward

327 W. Ninth St.
$32,500
2,748 sq. ft.
Lot 42 x 99

321 W. Ninth St.
$18,500
1,354 sq. ft.
Lot 58 x 99

427 N. Pine St.
$24,000
2,540 sq. ft.

Notice the "Rooms for Rent" sign. The damage from mildew and neglect is clearly visible, as are the empty lots on the street beyond the house. *Courtesy of Dennis Rash.*

Brevard Street houses prior to their move to Fourth Ward. *Courtesy of Catherine Barnhardt Browning.*

The Berryhill Foundation served as a matchmaker between empty lots in Fourth Ward, old houses that were in developing areas and were slated for demolition and prospective buyers. They also coordinated the moves with the various utilities, traffic managers and the movers themselves.

Many areas of Charlotte were experiencing rapid changes, not just Uptown. On Brevard Street in Dilworth, two homes were in the path of a new YMCA. While they sat beside each other originally, there were no adjacent sites available for them in Fourth Ward.

The Berryhill Foundation moved them to their new lots on opposite sides of Pine Street. They now sit at 506 and 601 North Pine Street.

> *There were two houses next to the YMCA that were moved to Pine Street, across the street from Alexander Michael's—on the same side as the Overcarsh House. We had to move those houses in the middle of the night because of traffic.*
>
> *One of those houses was going to a guy who was blind, and he walked with his house all the way. It was his house, and he wanted to be part of it. It took the night, but he did it.*
>
> —*Catherine Barnhardt Browning*

The gingerbread trim on the porches is as unique as a fingerprint. Even typical middle-class family homes built in this era would have fanciful exterior trim such as this.

On the night of the house move, the new owner of 506 North Pine walked with the house for much of the journey. He was going blind due to diabetes but was determined to participate in the move. Because the houses were moved at such a slow pace, he was able to walk beside the moving truck as it brought the house to Fourth Ward. At the new site, all of the planting beds in the surrounding yard were raised up to make it easier for him to garden by touch and scent as he lost his sight.

The ornamentation of these houses is a good example of what came to be known as the Charlotte style. The window at the center of the façade, the stained glass over the front window and the details at the gable and eaves near the bowed section show the care and craftsmanship of the builder.

Shown here at the original location at 712 North Pine Street, the house was in the path of the exit ramp for the new highway encircling Uptown Charlotte. *Courtesy of Catherine Barnhardt Browning.*

Above: This house is at a midway point in its journey to a new location. Notice that in this image, the surrounding lots are scrubby growth, easily cleared for the house's move. Part of the reason it was possible to relocate houses within Fourth Ward was the emptiness of the area. Because there were no other structures blocking the path, this house could be moved across the empty block between Pine and Poplar Streets and then along Poplar to its new site at the corner of Eighth and Poplar Streets. *Courtesy of Catherine Barnhardt Browning.*

Left: A different style is reflected in the beautiful Shaker shingle detail of the exterior and round windows of this Dutch Colonial. *Courtesy of Catherine Barnhardt Browning.*

Left: This Dutch Colonial would be moved to North Poplar Street. *Courtesy of Catherine Barnhardt Browning.*

Below: At 401 North Poplar Street, this small house was demolished to make room for the bootlegger's house to be moved onto the site. *Courtesy of Rufus Dalton.*

Opposite: Number 400 North Poplar, newly placed on the site, was sold by the Berryhill Foundation. The house has hidden cupboards and false backs to several closets, evidence of its history as a bootlegger's house. *Courtesy of Catherine Barnhardt Browning.*

These two houses attracted the Foundation on the strength of their architectural charm. The house now at the corner of Seventh and Poplar was sold to an architect, Mike Trent, who researched the home's history and uncovered a prior life as a bootlegger's refuge, complete with hidden compartments in the staircase and under the floorboards.

Number 316 West Ninth on its original Graham Street site. *Courtesy of Dennis Rash.*

The house that would become 428 North Poplar mid-move from the 700 block of Pine Street. Navigating the grade change between the center of the block and the street level was an extra challenge for this house. The highway encircling Uptown Charlotte is just behind the trees. *Courtesy of Catherine Barnhardt Browning.*

Number 316 West Ninth at its new site. This house clearly needs repair, but the quality of the building shows in the deep front porch, small consumption porch on the second floor and restrained decoration of the trim. *Courtesy of Catherine Barnhardt Browning.*

Number 316 West Ninth Street house still on the Crouch Brothers moving truck. The sign on the porch advertises furnished room for rent. *Courtesy of Catherine Barnhardt Browning.*

Above: Number 316 West Ninth being placed on new site. It was brought in from the rear of the lot, through what would soon become Settler's Lane. *Courtesy of Dennis Rash.*

Left: Number 513 North Pine was one of the few remaining original buildings in Fourth Ward. A sturdy house with a double porch and detached kitchen, it anchored the block as the empty lots around it filled with newly built and relocated homes. *Courtesy of Jim Renegar and Gloria Colltharp.*

The house that was moved to 316 West Ninth Street had actually been moved once before. While the original location is unclear, it was set on North Graham Street for several years before coming to this space as the final touch on the central block of rescued homes.

Sometimes the moves required creative thinking to make them fit. The house at 509 North Pine Street had to turn sideways to fit onto its new lot. The house was moved only one block, from 611 North Pine. It was the last of the Fourth Ward house moves managed by the Berryhill Foundation.

From 1977 to 1986, the Berryhill Foundation moved eight houses from around the county into Fourth Ward and several others into lots in Dilworth and Elizabeth.

4D The Charlotte News, Tuesday, July 19, 1983

4th Ward house moved for fix-up

By BETH ROGERS
OF THE NEWS STAFF

Last Tuesday was moving day — not for the contents of a house, but for the house itself.

It was only a short move — from 611 N. Pine St. to 509 N. Pine.

But it signaled an end: The house is the last single-family dwelling remaining to be restored in 4th Ward, the rejuvenated area northwest of The Square.

Berryhill Preservation Inc., the nonprofit group that buys, sells and sometimes moves houses in the interests of historic preservation, had the turn-of-the century house moved.

But while the organization was originally set up to help preservation efforts in 4th Ward, the event does not signal an end for Berryhill Preservation.

The organization is continuing its efforts elsewhere, said Catherine Barnhardt, the organization's immediate past president.

The organization, set up in 1976, decided two years ago to expand its efforts countywide.

While the group has only worked on one project outside 4th Ward and has no other immediate preservation plans, Mrs. Barnhardt said, "If something comes along, we are certainly available.

"We have not done anything in 4th Ward for quite a while (until the house move last week) simply because we didn't feel there was anything to do down there. . . .

"It's so exciting to go down there and look at what has taken place in a relatively short period of time."

Charlotte attorney Julius Chambers, who had bought the Pine Street house on its former lot from Malachi Greene, donated it to Berryhill Preservation.

He had planned to tear it down to make way for a duplex he and his physician brother, Kenneth, plan to build and live in.

But the Historic District Commission objected to tearing down the house.

So he donated it for moving.

The house, moved by Crouch Brothers House Moving Contractors Inc., now sits on its new lot, looking slightly naked, awaiting a new foundation and a new owner.

"All we do is move the house, put it on a foundation and sell it as is," said Mrs. Barnhardt, who is with Barnhardt Browning Residential Properties real estate firm.

She said the porch, dismantled for the move, will be reconstructed.

The house is being offered for sale at $59,500, "with very little profit built in," she said.

House sits on its new lot at 509 N. Pine St. (News photo/Jeep Hunter)

Berryhill Preservation, meanwhile, will keep looking for worthwhile efforts, said Mrs. Barnhardt, who was recently succeeded as president of the organization by architect Terry Shook.

"We'd like to be doing more than we are doing, but it's not easy to search out a good project," she said.

"We considered at one time closing shop," she said, "but decided we'd better keep functioning and be there when we' needed.

Interested persons can call Mrs. Barnhardt at 375-0445.

Number 509 North Pine had to be turned sideways to fit into its new location next to 513. *Courtesy of clipping from* Charlotte Observer.

Using the model that the Foundation created, several individual families also moved their homes. Four of these were moved to the block adjoining the Berryhill House, one on Pine Street and three along Ninth Street. This block had been almost empty, but the anchor structures on the corners remained: the Berryhill House at Ninth and Pine, the Sheppard House at Ninth and Poplar and the Poplar Apartment building at Tenth and Poplar. It was an ideal opportunity to create a solid center for the renewed neighborhood.

Among the early residents was the Rash family, Dennis and Marsha with their children Mebane and Jim. They were familiar with Uptown not only through Dennis's work but also because they attended First Presbyterian Church and because Marsha was deeply involved in the Junior League and the Berryhill House renovation.

> *We were driving home one day after church, and looking over from the highway* [Brookshire], *I saw the house. And I just thought, that might be such a beautiful thing if it were done right. And so we did it—we decided that we would move that one and redo it, and we did.*
>
> —*Marsha Rash Sherry*

This house would become the Rash family home at 320 West Ninth Street. Here it is seen on its original site as a front loader clears brush around it in preparation for the move. The neglected grounds, industrial lighting and empty lots surrounding the house are typical of the conditions in Fourth Ward at the time. *Courtesy of Dennis Rash.*

The Rash House on its original site, almost obscured by overgrowth and a burned-out van. *Courtesy of Catherine Barnhardt Browning.*

The Rash House looks a little bit better with most of the overgrowth cleared. The highway in background and the dearth of houses around it make the house look pretty lonely. *Courtesy of Catherine Barnhardt Browning.*

The house she had seen was a handsome three-story frame house. When the loop highway (Highway 277) was built around Charlotte, the house was spared, but the site was surrounded by the highway, its entrance and exit ramps and land zoned for commercial development. The house was slated for demolition.

Using the program that he had helped create at the bank, Dennis and Marsha Rash purchased the house and the empty lot adjacent to the Berryhill House. Crouch Brothers moved the house from the corner of Tenth and Graham Street to 320 West Ninth Street.

In the images of the Rash House during its move, notice the highway ramp in the left background. The proximity of the grand house and the traffic explains the need for the relocation!

> *The process of moving the house was incredible, and after we got it into the new lot, we found a corner cabinet in the dining room that had never been emptied out. It was full of juice glasses, and every one was still on the shelf!*
>
> *—Marsha Rash Sherry*

The emptiness of the surrounding blocks and the highway exit ramp in the rear are almost as surprising as seeing the Rash House (320 West Ninth Street) during its move. *Courtesy of Dennis Rash.*

The Rash House on the move from the corner of Tenth and Graham Street to 320 West Ninth Street. *Courtesy of Dennis Rash.*

The Rash House at its original site with steel girders inserted underneath the foundation for moving. *Courtesy of Dennis Rash.*

In order to move the houses, all of the electric and telephone lines along the route had to be taken down. The house's proximity to the ADM grain silos in the background gives an idea of some of the changes that the area had endured, from genteel homes to heavy industrialization. *Courtesy of Dennis Rash.*

The Rash House just before the move. It is on the truck with the ADM plant in the background. *Courtesy of Dennis Rash.*

Passing a gas station, the Manse moves from the industrial side of Graham. Street into the residential area. The process of moving the houses was painfully slow and required enormous coordination. It also generated huge excitement among those lucky enough to witness it. *Courtesy of Dennis Rash.*

Here, the Rash House turns the corner at Tenth Street. Notice the industrial feel of the streetscape's lighting and sidewalks. Seeing a house in the middle of the road must have been quite a shock! *Courtesy of Dennis Rash.*

These houses are a great example of all of the renovation activity happening in Fourth Ward in 1975. The Berryhill House was underway, with the porch railings removed and some of the foundation brick repairs completed. The Rash home at 320 West Ninth is still on the steel beams and truck bed after its move to the site. Two more homes would soon be moved in next to the Rash home, between it and the Sheppard House seen at the far right. *Courtesy of Dennis Rash.*

So many changes all at once were happening when this home was settled onto the site at 506 North Pine Street. Berryhill volunteer Jim Smith seems pleased with it and with the new infill construction going up next door. The new homes built in the 1970s were usually in a very modern style, in strong contrast to their older neighbors. The theory was that such a contrast would show the best of both styles, but it can seem an odd pairing. *Courtesy of Catherine Barnhardt Browning.*

Cullie and Sylvia Tarleton were thrilled to buy their new/old house and move it to the lot at 312 West Ninth Street. Cullie worked at WBT television station and had friends and colleagues who were also interested in the neighborhood. Although the area was rough, the house itself was beautifully proportioned, with high ceilings and well-preserved woodwork.

Seeing the Tarleton House (now at 312 West Ninth) on its original site surrounded by weeds and dirt is almost shocking.

This house would become the Tarleton home at 312 West Ninth Street. The partially collapsed chimney, broken windows and sagging porch don't obscure the charm of fanciful woodwork at the front door or the diamond-pattern window on the third floor. To support the weight of the house during the move, Crouch Brothers Company would excavate openings in the foundation to insert two or three steel beams along the length of the building. They would then back the truck (or trucks in this case) up and under the beams, clearing the old foundation as they progressed. Finally, the hydraulic truck beds would be raised and lift the house off the old foundation. *Courtesy of Dennis Rash.*

Top: The small diamond-pattern window on the Tarleton house, here before its move to 312 West Ninth, is almost the only way to recognize it. Its original lot became part of Fourth Ward Park. *Courtesy of Dennis Rash.*

Bottom: Loaded up on the trucks for the move, the house looks ready to roll. *Courtesy of Cullie and Sylvia Tarleton.*

Top: The Tarleton House on its old site with dirt removed from around the foundation to make room for the moving trucks. *Courtesy of Cullie and Sylvia Tarleton.*

Bottom: This photo shows the opposite side of Ninth Street viewed from the field that would become the Tarleton homesite. Untrimmed trees, scrub grass and boarded-up windows show how little care went into the area at the time. *Courtesy of Jim Renegar and Gloria Coltharp.*

Opposite, top: While the Tarleton House was awaiting its new foundation, construction was going on all around it. Notice the brickwork in progress in the foreground of this image. The building across the street had been a four-unit apartment house before conversion to a single-family home. The new owner, Jim Smith, enclosed part of the lot with the open brick wall to connect it to the home while giving some structure and privacy to a new garden. *Courtesy of Cullie and Sylvia Tarleton.*

Opposite, bottom: After the Tarleton home was placed on its new site at 312 West Ninth Street, a temporary support system was created between the beams and the new foundation. Cullie Tarleton was thinking of the long-term character of the homesite even as the movers were setting the house on the new lot. A moving truck bumped into the young tree in front of the house, nearly uprooting it. Cullie described shouting at the driver to stop and running over to tamp the soil back in place and straighten the trunk protectively. The movers thought he was overreacting, but the tree survived and became one of the family's favorite parts of their moving story. *Courtesy of Cullie and Sylvia Tarleton.*

Above: Here, the Tarleton House takes a rest at the corner of Ninth and Church Streets during its move. Shifting the houses was a logistical puzzle, sometimes done in the middle of the night or, as with this house, over a period of several days. *Courtesy of Cullie and Sylvia Tarleton.*

Here is the Tarleton home settling into its new foundation. To the left is another house that was recently moved; to the right is the rear of the Sheppard House. The concrete steps leading up from the sidewalk were from the prior house on the site and were replaced with handsome brick steps and bollards. *Courtesy of Cullie and Sylvia Tarleton.*

About one year after being moved, the Tarleton House boasts a cheery paint job, smart brickwork and a welcoming rebuilt porch. The landscaping is still quite young, including the tree that Cullie rescued during the move. The neighborhood is still growing, with the house next door newly settled on its foundation, and the condominiums on Settler's Street behind the house are under construction. *Courtesy of Cullie and Sylvia Tarleton.*

Harvey Gantt, an architect and city council member, decided to build a new home for his growing family in the neighborhood.

> *My parents were not too happy that I was moving the family into downtown. I grew up in downtown Charleston, and later my parents moved out of the city to the suburbs. That was a sign of success, of progress to them. They thought it was going backwards to move my kids from the green suburbs into the city.*
>
> —*Harvey Gantt*

He invited his friend Mel Watt to partner with him and build two new homes on adjoining lots on Poplar Street with a shared tennis court on the land behind them.

While some are surprised by the modern look of the homes, they were intentionally designed to stand in contrast to the Victorians, even as they

Harvey Gantt designed this house at 517 North Poplar Street for his family and the one next door for their friends Mel and Eulada Watt. The design of the homes uses many of the same elements as Gantt's commercial projects: large windows, natural materials, open spaces in the interior that allow light and air to flow through the rooms. *Courtesy of Jim Renegar and Gloria Coltharp.*

share elements such as front porches and pocket gardens. This allows both types of buildings to be true to their own character and creates an interesting rhythm in the streetscape.

Mel Watt related a conversation he and Harvey had as they were finalizing the plans for the houses. The families hadn't decided which lot each would have and needed to choose in order to move forward. Mel said that he didn't really have a preference, even as Harvey pressed for the decision.

> *Finally, Harvey said, "Just choose one or the other so we can get on with it! Do you want the one with the abandoned car or the one with the old refrigerator in it?" And that's how we decided who went where!*
>
> —*Mel Watt*

This house faces Church Street between Ninth and Eighth. At the right is the rear of the First United Methodist Church complex, which occupies half of the block. When a high-rise office building and luxury condominiums were to be built on the other half of the block, the house had to go. Luckily, Loy McKeithen was able to arrange for it to be moved to 326 West Tenth Street. He and Dennis Rash were developing other lots on Tenth Street as townhouses, and Loy used this house as his primary residence for a few years.

Opposite: The large house prepared to move from Church Street to Tenth Street. It is shown here mid-move, in the parking lot of the First Methodist Church. *Courtesy of Dennis Rash.*

Above: Overshadowed by the church, this house was moved to make way for a new condominium development. *Courtesy of Dennis Rash.*

The building at 522 Graham Street was once a beloved family home, but over the decades, it was converted into rental units and then a used clothing store. Graham Street was very rundown in the early 1970s, with a mix of light industrial sites, empty lots and old houses in disrepair. Notice the storage building to the left and the view of Edwin Towers, a full block and a half away.

The Berryhill Foundation purchased the house and the lot that adjoined it mid-block and faced Pine Street. The movers decided to move the building across that boundary instead of transporting it around the perimeter of the

Left: Settled onto its new site at 523 North Pine Street, the house looks a little bare. The Lowry family purchased it from the Berryhill Foundation. *Courtesy of Jim Renegar and Gloria Coltharp.*

Below: The house at 522 Graham Street has a wonderful Queen Anne design, with a turret and deeply shaded porch, but it had damage to the roof and missing windows by the time of this photo. *Courtesy of Dennis Rash.*

Number 522 Graham Street from a second angle. *Courtesy of Dennis Rash.*

A combination of beautiful detail and sad neglect can be seen in this home about to be moved. *Courtesy of Dennis Rash.*

block. The plan was to simply lift the house, rotate it 180 degrees and shift it about sixty feet to the new site. The company had moved larger houses greater distances, and this was not seen as a big move.

But when the house was lifted off the foundation, the moving company discovered that the kitchen addition was not fully attached to the house. As the building was being rotated, the kitchen actually broke away from the rest of the house! It had apparently been added onto the house rather shoddily, and the stress of the move destroyed it.

When the Lowry family purchased the home and considered options for reconstruction on the new site, they decided to use the first floor as office space for Gordon's company and to rebuild the kitchen as part of an apartment on the second floor.

As the neighborhood took shape, planners realized that clustering the houses and having a contiguous park space would be better than a series of small parks and scattered houses. The existing structures in the designated parkland were put up for sale with the stipulation that they had to move; the ones that didn't sell were torn down. Gail Fenimore, a new resident on Ninth Street, remembered the sad feeling of those blocks before the park began to take shape.

> *There were a few houses in the park when they started bringing that together, but there weren't very many at all, and they were kind of scattered.*
>
> *All along on Pine Street, there would be steps going up to houses that were long gone.*
>
> —*Gail Fenimore*

The Betty family's house was originally at the corner of Sixth and Pine Streets and was in poor condition. The lot on which it stood was designated for the Fourth Ward Park, and many thought that the house should simply be demolished. It had suffered from years of neglect and then from a fire started by squatters trying to stay warm. The interior damage was even worse. But the structure was sound, and under the soot, the interior details were beautiful.

Mebane Rash, Dennis and Marsha's daughter, was a curious elementary schooler when the houses were being evaluated and moved.

Even as the house was loaded up for relocation, it held together. One can clearly see extensive fire damage to the exterior and rot. *Courtesy of Dennis Rash.*

The fire-damaged house was set on a new foundation at 610 North Pine and stabilized for sale to the Betty family. Kimm Jolly of the Berryhill Foundation looks very pleased standing in front of the house after the basic repairs were completed. *Courtesy of Dennis Rash.*

I remember, Dad and I went around as this was starting and toured almost all the houses. One house was a Sears and Roebuck kit house that the Bettys were considering.

When Dad and I toured it, there had been a fire. You can see the remnants of the fire still on the banister, and when we walked in, he fell right through the floor and into the basement.

—Mebane Rash

The family decided it was worth saving and renovating; they purchased and moved it with the support of the Berryhill Foundation. The family decided to move it to the lot adjacent to the Berryhill House, near their friends, the Rash family.

Jim and Robin Cochran were among the first residents to build a new house on an empty lot on Eighth Street. Robin was familiar with the neighborhood from her work with the Junior League and the Berryhill House, and Jim was interested in creating a home where their two children could safely walk and play independently.

We lived on Wendover Road, and it was getting busy. But when I was down here working on the Berryhill, I would hear the train whistle going by, and it felt like a little mill village. That had a great appeal for us as a family. Jim didn't want to tackle an old house. This would be our third house, and we wanted to do something that was exciting and different.

The owner of that lot had torn the house down and moved away. This little lot was 50 feet wide and 150 feet deep. You could see the guy at the closing thinking, "There's a fool born every minute, and these dopes just took this off my hands." He really thought we were crazy to pay $15,000.

—Robin Cochran

Architect Ron Morgan incorporated then-novel elements of passive solar heating and seamless transitions to the enclosed garden. He also sited an open staircase and window with a special treat for the Cochran children.

Number 318 West Eighth Street, shown here under construction, was one of the first homes to be added to the neighborhood. *Courtesy of Robin Cochran.*

> *It was such fun working with Ron. He put in that diamond window, and when I asked him what is it for, he said it was so that the kids can see the moon. And they could!*
>
> —*Robin Cochran*

Rufus and Ruth Dalton were involved in Fourth Ward in several ways. Ruth had worked on the Berryhill and wanted to continue to be part of the action. She and her friend Catherine Belk purchased the old Berryhill Store at the

THURSDAY, MARCH 22, 1979—MOORESVILLE (N.C.) TRIBUNE—9

The Granddaddy Of All Mobile Homes

This road full of house was on U. S. 21 just south of N. C. 150 at mid-morning Friday. It was on its way to Charlotte to begin a new life among other restored homes in the Fourth Ward. Crouch Bros. of Mooresville moved the first floor of the 90-year-old W. W. Rankin homeplace from the 300 block of South Broad Street for its owners, Mr. and Mrs. Rufus Dalton. The second story was disassembled, and it will be replaced after the house is positioned in its new location. The movers began hauling the house at 5 a.m. Friday. They moved north on South Broad to Iredell, out Iredell to Plaza Drive, west on Plaza Drive to River Road (N. C. 150), and out to U.S. 21. With a Highway Patrol escort, the house was taken south on U.S. 21 to Crouch Bros.' office north of Charlotte near the Metrolina Fairgrounds. It will be placed this week on the Fourth Ward lot being prepared for it.

Left: "Mobile home" got a new meaning when this house was moved from Mooresville to Fourth Ward. The novelty of the project made great press for the local papers and helped keep up enthusiasm and interest in the reading public. *Courtesy of clipping from* Mooresville Times.

Below: The aftermath of the fire at 420 North Poplar. The fire department said that they were lucky to save the adjacent houses because the old wood burned so fast and hot. *Courtesy of Alsop family*.

opposite corner from the Berryhill House and the two small mill houses on either side of it.

Rufus's family business was in Mooresville, North Carolina, about thirty miles away, but he and Ruth lived on the southern side of Charlotte. When he learned that an old house in Mooresville was to be torn down for new development, Rufus and Ruth purchased it to move into Fourth Ward as their new family home.

Ruth was very involved with the planning, move and renovation; she had detailed architectural drawings made of the house before the move to ensure that every element was preserved.

> *She just loved that house and was so excited about it. She had all the plans and was up there all the time that the work was going on.*
>
> *And then one night, we got a call from one of the neighbors in Fourth Ward that there was a fire at the house. We jumped in the car and drove up there. As soon as we made that turn from Trade Street onto Poplar, we could see the flames shooting up and all the smoke. It was just awful.*
>
> *When we got closer and could really see what was left of the house, Ruth just looked at me and said, "Well I guess we're never moving to Fourth Ward."*
>
> —*Rufus Dalton*

The house on the right of the fire at 416 North Poplar had only recently been moved to the site and was still boarded up awaiting its new owners. *Courtesy of Alsop family.*

Above: Only the newly rebuilt chimneys and foundation of 420 North Poplar remained after the fire. The house to the left of the burned house had extensive damage. In addition to the damage from the fire, notice the clear view of Edwin Towers, almost two blocks away. Today, the area is one of the most densely populated in Greater Charlotte, but in 1980, the neighborhood was still taking shape on a mostly blank canvas. *Courtesy of Dennis Rash.*

Left: The view from the middle of the block after the fire at 420 North Poplar. *Courtesy of Dennis Rash.*

Ruth was heartbroken over the loss of the house, and the fire was later determined to have been caused by vagrants who lit a fire in one of the still-closed fireplaces. The house's timber was so old and dry that it was demolished before the firemen could do much to save it.

Because they had the architectural plans for the house, Rufus decided to rebuild it in hopes that they could still move in one day. But even after the reconstruction, Ruth declined to move; the fire had really taken the sense of fun out of the project for her. The Daltons sold the house and, soon after, sold the commercial properties, too.

The Berryhill Foundation continued to move houses into the neighborhood as long as there were open lots available in the residential core.

By 1986, the Berryhill Foundation and private owners had moved a total of fourteen houses into empty lots within the boundaries of Fourth Ward. While these relocated neighbors often blend seamlessly with the original homes, one can sometimes spot a "transplant." Look for homes where the foundation is a different material than the main structure or ones with a double-height foundation, as on West Ninth Street.

> *Everyone was at the right age to make it all work; we weren't just babies, but we had energy and could plunge in and do it. We had a little money, but not much, and we were young enough to be a little blind about it. And we attracted other people who wanted to be part of it and plunged in. I don't know how everyone got here, but they came!*
>
> —*Robin Cochran*

One of the most common things these urban homesteaders said in their interviews was that they felt they were "circling the wagons" in their little community. On first hearing this, one might be a bit dismayed that it indicates that they felt threatened by their surroundings. What becomes clear with these stories is that it was instead a commitment to community (one resident even called it a commune) and was more about creating a deep connection among the neighbors than what was happening beyond its boundaries.

They wanted to be part of a village and set about creating it.

RENOVATING THE NEIGHBORHOOD

As vital as the preservation of the Berryhill House and the other houses were, a neighborhood-wide renovation was needed, too. Without the extraordinary vision and commitment of numerous institutions, those homes would be beautiful buildings surrounded by blight. As homeowners and the Berryhill Foundation worked on individual sites, other community members continued to raise awareness of the benefits of preservation in general and Fourth Ward in particular.

In parallel to those efforts, leaders within Bank of America and local governments brought institutional support to big projects in and around the neighborhood. They intentionally and diligently created the structures needed for a viable neighborhood with owner-occupied homes.

With the encouragement of the *Charlotte Observer* and other community organizers, their combined efforts allowed the community to grow and thrive.

The *Charlotte Observer*

Rolfe Neill was the publisher of the *Charlotte Observer* and an advocate for the appreciation of the region's historic assets. He served on the board of the Berryhill Foundation and was interested in getting other people interested in the development potential he saw in Fourth Ward.

Moving In

Here it comes — Ty Betty's new home. Betty watches as the house turns off Poplar St. between Ninth and 10th streets on its way to its new location on Pine St. behind the restored, 19th century Berryhill home. The house is one of several being moved into Fourth Ward, a downtown area now undergoing renovation. (News staff photo by Jeep Hunter)

Above: The novelty of houses being moved about like puzzle pieces made good press. The coverage of the moves, such as this image of Tyson Betty watching his house move up what would become Settler's Lane, was a frequent feature of the *Observer*. The house at the right is the Shepard House, one of the original Victorian homes that remains in its original location. *Courtesy of Jim Renegar and Gloria Coltharp.*

Left: A coloring page that was published by the Berryhill Foundation as a children's contest. It ran in numerous papers in the region and attracted about one hundred entries. *Courtesy of George Breisacher.*

The goings-on in Fourth Ward made good footage for local news channels, and many future residents came to the area after seeing a story on the rapidly changing neighborhood. *Courtesy of Dennis Rash.*

> *I couldn't be too obvious about it, couldn't take sides really. But I did try to keep my foot on the gas for the project, and people knew that I was involved as a volunteer for the Foundation and that I kept up with Fourth Ward. So, it happened that the neighborhood was mentioned in the paper quite often.*
>
> —*Rolfe Neill*

Neill knew that the novelty of houses being moved about like puzzle pieces would appeal to readers. The paper even supported the efforts by publishing a coloring page for kids to complete and mail in for a chance to have their artwork featured in the newspaper.

CITIZENS FOR PRESERVATION

Patsy Kinsey, Mary Pickens and Kimm Jolly were quintessential civic volunteers. They each had helped at their children's schools, served on PTAs and supported local library activities. They discovered a shared preservation

9.

523 North Poplar Street

This house is in good condition. It has the typically Victorian wrap-around porch and two-over-two window panes.

10.

529 North Poplar Street

This is another typical "turn-of-the-century" house. It has a patterned slate roof and good sturdy lines that make one feel the house, barring the wrecking-ball, will stand another 70 odd years.

Left: This page from *Stained Glass and Gingerbread* is typical of the booklet—simple, straightforward and optimistic. *Courtesy of Ed Perzel.*

Right: Patsy Kinsey began working with Citizens for Preservation as a volunteer in the early 1970s. Seen here in front of Overcarsh House in about 1975, she went on to become a tireless advocate for Charlotte's historic assets as a member of city council. *Courtesy of Catherine Barnhardt Browning.*

interest, although none had a professional background in history or architecture. The rampant demolition of old buildings for new development struck them as simply wasteful and shortsighted, and they were among the founders of the grassroots group Citizens for Preservation (CFP), which sought to slow the pace of destruction.

By documenting the assets for the community and relentlessly advocating for preservation, CFP played an instrumental role in saving Fourth Ward.

UNC CHARLOTTE HISTORY DEPARTMENT

Ed Perzel and Dan Morrill were both new professors in the History Department at UNC Charlotte. They had an academic interest in the local historic assets and found common cause with the Citizens for Preservation folks. Ed joined the group, while Dan focused on research that would support their message. Both men thought the prospect of getting Charlotteans excited about their own history was great fun and could be an interesting way of engaging the city.

> *When I walked around Fourth Ward, I thought it was kind of cool…and then we started talking with the CFP people and realized that we could probably get a grant to help with their research and turn it into something with academic quality.*
>
> *Then we discovered that groups around town wanted to hear about it, so we could go and talk with this or that club…spread the word and make a little money on the side! As a junior teacher on a pretty low salary, I found that all pretty interesting.*
>
> —*Ed Perzel*

BANK OF AMERICA

Supporting the Berryhill House renovation was just the start of the relationship between the bank* and Fourth Ward. The bank provided the bulk of initial funding for the Junior League's purchase of the Berryhill House in October 1975, but the vision for Fourth Ward was much grander than just a single house renovation. Under the stewardship of Hugh McColl, Dennis Rash and Joe Martin, the bank made a commitment to provide not only steady funding but also the personnel and political backing to support the rebirth of the area as a residential haven.

McColl often repeated the mantra "You can't have a great bank without a great city," and Rash convinced him that housing had to be part of the center city fabric.

> *I'd made up my mind early on that we needed to bring in talent to make the bank. We needed to be able to attract people from big cities to our town. That's why I was so intent on the development of the arts and housing and sports. It wasn't really about making money. It was about getting these people to come.*
>
> —*Hugh McColl*

* A note on nomenclature: During most of the time discussed in this book, the core of the institution that is today Bank of America was known as North Carolina National Bank. After a series of mergers, it was renamed NationsBank in 1992; after an acquisition in 1998, it took the name Bank of America. For clarity, it will generally be called Bank of America, except where a quoted source uses a different name.

This is the view looking north from the executive office floor at the Bank of America Tower in approximately 1980. At the lower left of the photo is Settler's Cemetery, with the North Carolina Medical College Building adjoining it at the corner of Sixth and North Church Streets. The prevalence of parking lots and empty lots in Fourth Ward is the most noticeable feature of the city scape at the time. *Courtesy of Dennis Rash.*

Aerial view up College Street to Seventh Street when these blocks were dominated by parking lots. *Courtesy of Dennis Rash.*

Aerial view to the north. The rail line bisects left to right; Elmwood Cemetery is top center; the Federal Courthouse is lower right. *Courtesy of Dennis Rash.*

Aerial view of Fourth Ward. The only buildings visible in Fourth Ward are the Poplar Apartments and Edwin Towers. The rest is parking lots and forest cover. *Courtesy of Dennis Rash.*

When McColl looked out his office window over Fourth Ward and the northern part of Uptown, it was shockingly empty, either green lots or parking lots.

The question of how the bank could support a range of housing options was tricky because it wasn't a standard part of the bank's operations. Lending to developers or individual owners was traditional but would not produce the interconnected fabric of a neighborhood. Rash was convinced that the best solution would be for the bank to be directly involved with creating a mixture of market and affordable housing and demonstrating a long-term commitment to slow and steady growth. This approach, coupled with a design review process for the whole district, would support a cohesive character for the neighborhood.

From his experience in real estate law, Rash understood the new urban planning tools being deployed in historic downtowns around the country. Cities around the country were increasingly recognizing that 1950s and '60s "urban renewal" efforts that razed older or blighted neighborhoods were not effectively addressing the deep problems of their core. They saw, too, that the resources still extant in stressed neighborhoods could be used to spark a different type of renewal. Cities began experimenting with development loans and community development corporations. At the state and national level, the concept of historic districts was developed to recognize areas that had special significance. Preservationists organized grant programs and educational efforts to promote saving older buildings and neighborhoods, as well as the community structures that they supported.

Successful efforts in these cities tended to have areas with numerous, well-preserved and concentrated historic buildings. Without those assets, it was clear that what worked in Charleston, Savannah and San Francisco had to be modified to succeed in Charlotte.

> *What was intriguing about the process from the city's perspective…they couldn't figure out what their proper role was.*
>
> *Having had a lot of tax law at UVA,* [I was interested in] *the mechanism that Norfolk was using to borrowing money from Manufacturers Hanover. So, I looked into the North Carolina general statutes and saw that if we had historic districts, we would have a legitimate connection to establish* [tax] *deductibility, and it would make sense for a bank to get into this.*
>
> —*Dennis Rash*

Numbers 607 and 609 North Pine Street are in poor condition, with vacant lots stretching out behind them to the highway. Number 609 was torn down shortly after this image was taken. *Courtesy of Catherine Barnhardt Browning.*

Numbers 607 and 609 North Pine Street from the garden of the Berryhill House as Junior League volunteers work to clean up the site. *Courtesy of Dennis Rash.*

Rash saw the opportunity for the city and local banks to form a partnership to finance the real estate development that they wanted to incentivize. By approaching the issues using financing, zoning and tax law tools, the bank and the local governments would be able to set a new course for the redevelopment of the neighborhood.

Partnering with the Local Governments

The City of Charlotte had considered employing eminent domain measures to take control of Fourth Ward, but so many properties were empty of structures that it did not qualify as blighted for those standards. The city and Mecklenburg County staff had also suggested a National Register District designation as a tool for preservation, but the Fourth Ward was too fragmented to qualify for that status. The North Carolina State Office of Culture (SOC) reviewed the city's initial proposals and agreed that the area was not eligible for the National Register. However, the SOC suggested that the area might qualify as a local historic district, a new concept in North Carolina. With this validation, civic leaders sought and received the ability to create local districts from the North Carolina state legislature in 1976.

Dennis Rash was part of that lobbying effort. He recognized that, as a certified historic district, the Fourth Ward would qualify for loans with a special tax treatment, giving banks an economic incentive to make the loans. From the bank, he and Joe Martin worked with city and county leadership and other community members to get Fourth Ward designated as a historic district, Charlotte's first.

The Historic District Commission (HDC) was created by city council in 1976 with "the purpose of encouraging the restoration, preservation and conservation of historically significant areas, structures, sites or objects with the district."*

One striking element of the government agencies' involvement in the redevelopment of the Fourth Ward was their willingness to recognize that the "normal" tools were wrong for this project. Senior city planners had come through the era of urban renewal that used widescale demolition of structures in targeted areas. This heavy-handed technique was widely seen as too blunt a tool for true renewal; the community fabric was destroyed along with the physical assets. In Charlotte's Second Ward, the African American neighborhood of Brooklyn had been effectively eliminated in the late 1960s. Businesses, homes and schools were razed, and the resulting dislocation and fracturing of the social support network was profound.

Reflecting on that experience, city leadership was eager to approach Fourth Ward differently:

> *Walter Phillips, Assistant Director of Community Development stated the first hearing today is on Fourth Ward. That as an introduction to the Fourth Ward Amendment, he would give a brief history of the events leading up to the preparation of the amendment. He stated as the Community Development Department Staff got into the implementation of this project* **it became obvious that they could not proceed with their normal method of buying property, demolishing structures, designing public improvements, etc.—that they had a different animal on their hands.** *As a result of a detailed analysis, it was decided to contract with a landscape architectural firm with previous experience of historic preservation and design of public improvements for historic districts. That one of the requirements of the contract was to produce a master plan for Fourth Ward—this master plan, among other things, was to produce a more detailed study of land use,*

* City of Charlotte City Council, meeting minutes from May 3, 1976.

> *zoning, streets patterns, public improvements and a realistic guide for future development, as well as conservation of significant or usable structures.**

This master plan signaled a fundamental shift in philosophy of the city's approach to land use and development in the neighborhood and the surrounding blocks of Uptown.

First, it authorized the HDC and Community Development staff to actively engage with the neighborhood instead of simply waiting for projects to be brought to them for approval. The plan was designed to be more useful and accessible for homeowners in several ways. It clarified the HDC guidelines for changes to properties in the district and phrased the rules in language meant for homeowners instead of architects and design professionals. The city centralized the approval process at the HDC, whereas property owners wanting to make changes previously had to navigate sometimes conflicting regulations from various city agencies. The layman's language of the revised guidelines paired with the centralized process of working with the HDC for approvals were a huge improvement, and the HDC staff became valued partners to the neighborhood's residents as they figured out how to build the physical structure of the community.

Second, the plan prioritized adding public facilities, quasi-public and open space. It eliminated office space as a promoted land use; while property owners could develop their site as offices, the city would not work to advance that particular use. This shift in priorities set aside the land to create Fourth Ward Park, consolidating open space, allowing for sound existing structures to be moved and budgeting for improvements to the site.

Third, the master plan called for a shift from accommodating autos and trucks to a focus on promoting pedestrian traffic. The initial changes were aesthetic: cement sidewalks and industrial lights were replaced with brick walkways, granite curbs and old-fashioned lighting throughout the historic district. While these made walking more pleasant, additional changes were needed to make walking safe. From Highway 277, interstate traffic exited directly into Fourth Ward at the intersection of Tenth and Pine Streets. To access the Uptown business district, eighteen-wheeled tractor trailers often barreled through these narrow streets at near-highway speeds, creating a dangerous conflict with residents.

The closure of several streets at various points in Fourth Ward was one of the most impactful changes for the residents.

* City of Charlotte City Council, meeting minutes from July 10, 1978.

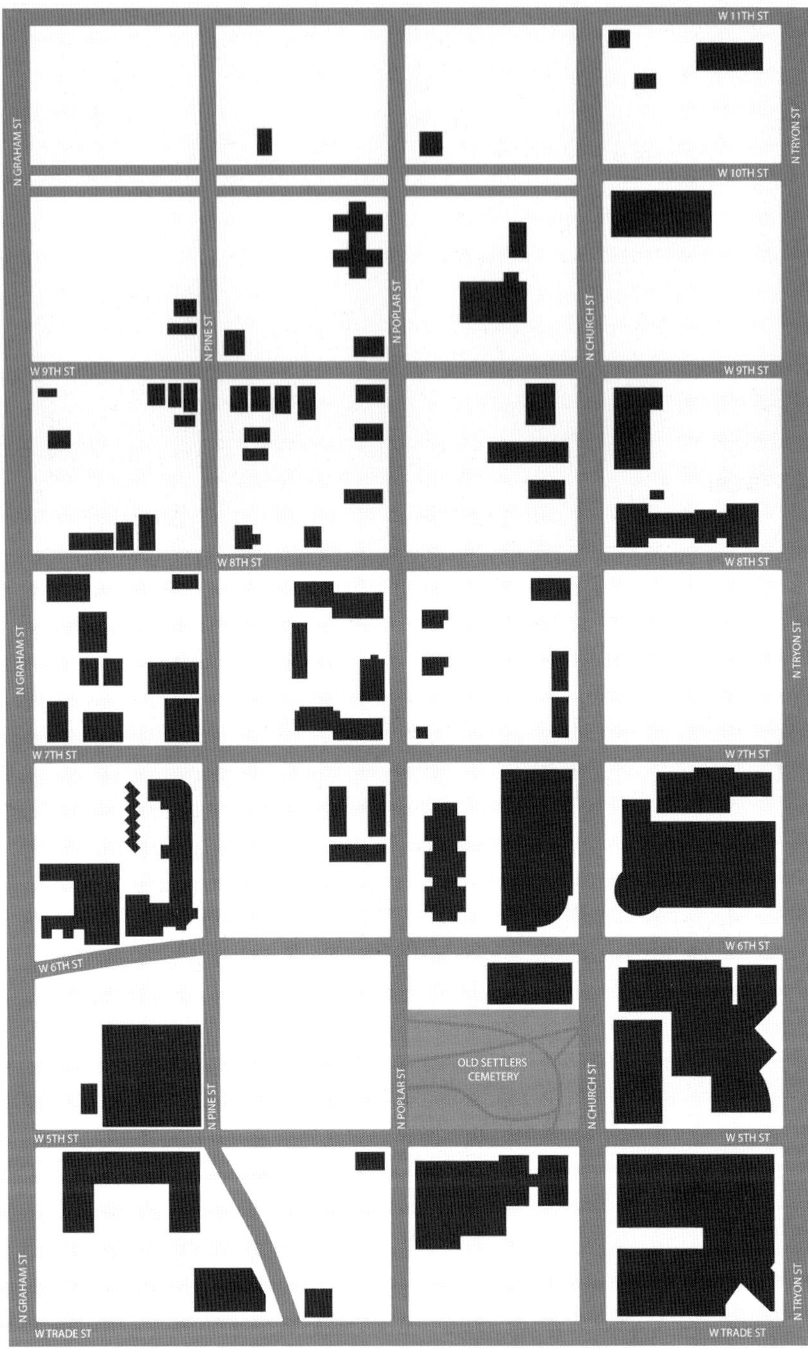

Fourth Ward in 1975. *Map by Gau Gupta, modified by the author.*

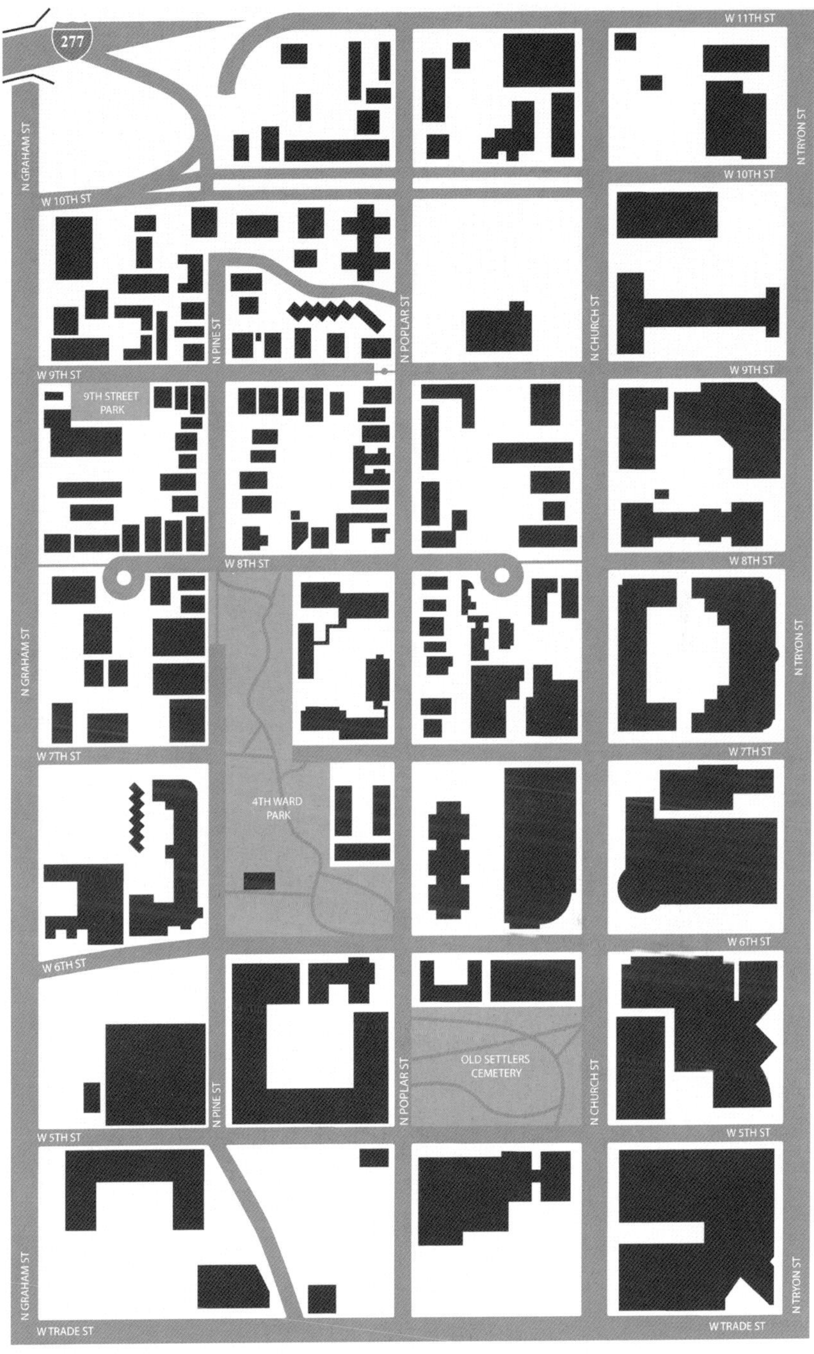

Fourth Ward in 2023. *Map by Gau Gupta, modified by the author.*

It took many months for large-vehicle drivers to accept and adapt to the changes, even after the city erected signs and temporary barriers across the roads where closings would soon come.

> *Every morning on the way to the office I'd put the barriers back where someone had moved them aside overnight...and every afternoon when I came home, I'd do it again because somebody had moved them during the day!*
>
> —*Tom Fenimore*

The master plan emphasized walkability, residential scale and access to city amenities. These features would come to be hallmarks of life in Fourth Ward.

Lastly, the city would no longer assemble property for private developers. By announcing that it was stepping back from this role in the Fourth Ward, the city made clear its preference for more organic and transparent development efforts.

The city council, county commission and their staff's willingness to work in tandem with architects, residents, community interest groups and developers had the effect of enhancing the impact of each contributor.

The Community Development Corporation

While the primary purpose of the HDC was to establish and enforce design guidelines for the neighborhood, its creation also enabled the bank and the City of Charlotte to create a Community Development Corporation (CDC) to pursue direct real estate development ventures.

> *We don't need to spend a lot of time and energy building a domestic neighborhood and then have some tacky fast-food joint in the middle of it.*
>
> —*Dennis Rash*

In early 1975, Dennis made the pitch to McColl for a CDC that could manage a pool of money to be lent in support of projects in Fourth Ward. The bank could lend the funds to the City of Charlotte (thus qualifying for tax breaks); the city would place the funds with the CDC; and the CDC would make and supervise loans in the historic district. Because the CDC was managing the loans, they could have benefits and restrictions unlike those of traditional loans. First, these preservation loans were made at a 6½

Community Development Corporation sign in center of vast empty lots, on Poplar Street between Eighth and Seventh. *Courtesy of Catherine Barnhardt Browning.*

percent annual interest rate, an extraordinarily low cost when the prevailing interest rate was close to 10 percent.* Second, the loans required that the home mortgage borrowers actually reside at the mortgaged property. Last, the loans stipulated a balloon payment of the outstanding principal after fifteen years.

> *I went in and said, we need a mortgage fund, so we need somebody to lend to the city 3 to 5 million. And Hugh, what I really need is somebody in the bank that will care and care actively and will lead me and others around the barriers in the bank.*
>
> *He said that the money is the easy part. The person will be really important—I think you should work with this fellow Joe Martin.*
>
> —*Dennis Rash*

* In 1976, standard thirty-year mortgages were offered with an interest rate of about 9.5 percent. Rates peaked at 18.4 percent in October 1981 and remained in the mid-teens through the 1980s.

Joe Martin was part of the bank's government and community relations team. He was able to understand the positive multiplier effect that investing in Fourth Ward would produce, lifting the neighborhood and city around it while also enhancing the bank's reputation as a good civic citizen. Martin became the leading advocate for the CDC and the development process within the bank while Rash led the CDC.

And they stayed in the effort for the long term. In addition to being the primary source of lending for the CDC, the bank became a developer in its own right. Dennis identified several parcels of land that were good candidates for new construction; especially interesting was the property on the block between Ninth and Tenth, Poplar and Pine Streets.

Residential owners were moving houses onto the Ninth Street side of the block, but the rest of the block was empty. To take advantage of the full space, Dennis conceived a new street to wind through the block and allow for townhouses on small lots.

He approached Edwin Jones of JA Jones Construction, which owned the Poplar Apartments and the adjacent, empty plots. The Jones company had numerous holdings in the Fourth Ward and was ready to divest of them as the market changed. Jones countered that he would not sell the few plots that Rash wanted unless the deal included all of the empty lots the company held on Poplar between Ninth and Eight Streets. Although that was not part of Dennis's original plan, he was able to get approval for it and agreed to the price. Jones introduced a new twist:

> *When he saw that we were capable of doing that, he said okay, then you have to buy the Poplar too. And that was what I really wanted all along! That was what we were angling for. I was as happy as Brer Rabbit in the briar patch!*
>
> *—Dennis Rash*

Adding the Poplar Apartment building to the project gave the CDC a steady, though small, income stream from the rents and allowed it to have full control of the site. In September 1978, NCNB announced that it would spend $3.5 million to acquire and renovate the Poplar Apartment building and develop the surrounding area. It created a new street, Settler's Place, which winds through the middle of the block and allows access to new condominium sites.

Renovating the Poplar Building was a multiyear effort, and it brought the CDC into the neighborhood in a new way. Many of the Poplar's residents were elderly and low-income, and they received rental assistance from

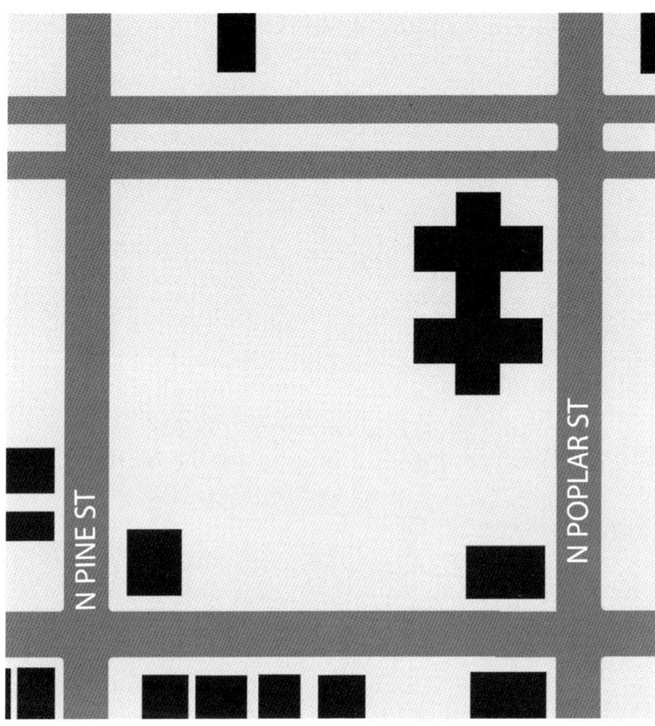

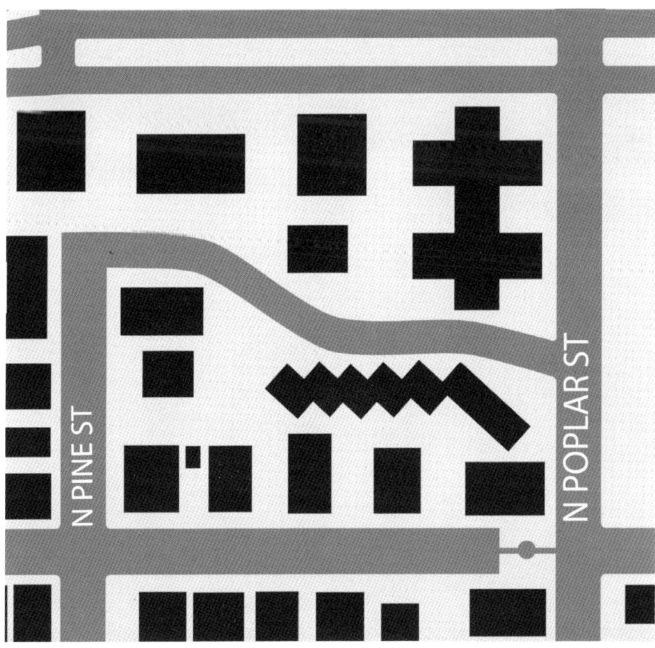

Top: The block between Ninth and Tenth, Poplar and Pine Streets was almost completely remade during the renovation of the neighborhood. In 1975, there were few extant buildings, and the highway off-ramp emptied directly onto Pine Street. There were no stop signs on Pine between Tenth Street and Sixth Street, so truck and car traffic was very heavy and fast. *Bottom*: The same block after changes to the street arrangements and new construction. Closing access to Pine Street from Tenth Street helped calm all the traffic through the area. Creating the new street, Settler's Lane, through the mid-block gave space for townhouses built with a relationship to the pedestrian-friendly sidewalks. *Map by Gau Gupta, modified by the author.*

Charlotte Housing Authority. The CDC made a commitment that residents would never be forced to move.

> *Forcing anyone out would have set a tone of exclusivity instead of inclusivity. And to me that inclusivity is what the neighborhood was all about, the "urban stew." And stews don't get better from just a couple of ingredients.*
>
> —*Dennis Rash*

When a resident was ready to relocate from the Poplar, the staff at the CDC would help them find their next apartment. Edwin Towers, built by the Charlotte Housing Authority in 1966, became one of their preferred destinations. As a modern mid-rise tower of subsidized housing, it had many advantages over the aging apartments, and it was just across Poplar Street from the apartment building, allowing people to stay in the neighborhood even as it (and they) changed.

Using this framework for transitioning residents over time, the CDC was able to renovate the Poplar building gradually, as units became available, and sell the refurbished units at market rates as they were completed. The smaller scale and slower pace allowed the group to manage the project themselves and to bring contractors and tradespeople into the site with a smaller, revolving budget.

> *We needed time, so we bought time. But it was a nightmare inside—originally thirty-nine units and it had been chopped into fifty-three. There were places where if you wanted to change the breaker on the second floor you had to go up to the seventh floor to get to it.*
>
> —*Dennis Rash*

While the Poplar Building was being updated, the CDC began construction to convert the vacant portion of the block into a new street and townhouses. The design of Settler's Place pulled inspiration from many of Dennis's favorite places: the brick facades of Boston's Beacon Hill, the porches of Charleston, the jewel-box gardens of London. It also carved out a service alley behind the townhouses and created a large, shared garden with a heritage hackberry tree tucked amid the private lots.

In designing the townhouses, the CDC sought to convey high quality in every element of the building design and construction. Units had to have parking while keeping the focus on neighborhood walkability. There had to be connection to the street without making residents feel too vulnerable.

Southern Living's feature and cover photo in the November 1980 issue were an important public relations coup. *Author's collection.*

Generously scaled porches face the street from a second level, above a garage; sitting on the porch, a resident can feel connected to the streetscape but not too exposed. Rooms have large windows that frame the views. The buildings have thick walls, solid doors, good hardware, wrought-iron railings with an open pattern.

The units relate well to each other and to the street, but they aren't so close that they, or their residents, lose privacy or individual identity.

Settler's Place also created a housing option for new neighbors who wanted something smaller and more affordable than a standalone house that needed renovation. Many of the new condo owners were single women who had been seeking a way into the neighborhood without having to take on the risk and exposure of a full house.

The development was a huge success for the bank. It brought accolades from national press, and the financial returns allowed the CDC to justify taking on more projects. It also became the model that the bank would embrace to build or renovate additional residential communities.

While technically independent of the bank, the CDC was closely tied to the institution, and they often worked hand-in-glove to ensure that the changing neighborhood reflected the bank's goals for the city.

> *The fundamental difference is that XYZ Corp comes in, buys a piece of land and builds here and then goes forty blocks away and builds another development, but they don't stay.*
>
> *Fourth Ward was* our *neighborhood. So, we care about what happens five streets away and ten streets away, and five and ten years down the road.*
>
> —*Hugh McColl*

Friends of Fourth Ward

More people coming to live in Fourth Ward and increased attention to the growth of the area led stakeholders to look for ways to collaborate on their common goals.

> [We needed an organization for] *contending with things like the city permits and getting lights put up and the street changes and the sidewalks.*
>
> *The neighborhood association* [Friends of Fourth Ward] *grew out of Jim Smith's organization skills. He was a lawyer, so he drew up the paperwork, and I was the first president. Because there was hardly anybody living here, it was made up of all the people who were hoping to come here or who were working on things here.*
>
> *We worked with the district commission and with the city planner. Getting the Fourth Ward Park done was a big thing.*
>
> —*Tom Fenimore*

There was continuing support from the bank for the development of the neighborhood, continuing enthusiasm among the women who had worked on the Berryhill and continuing interest in the story of the rehabilitation buoyed by the local paper and grassroots activism. These were essentially the three pillars of the endeavor; each was necessary but not sufficient.

AMATEURS WITH POWER TOOLS

Renovating Individual Homes

While the neighborhood needed all of the civic and corporate support described in the prior chapters, the individual people and families who decided to live here really brought the collection of buildings to life as a neighborhood. In Fourth Ward, the new residents brought a commitment to being in community as well as the desire to make their individual houses into homes.

Many of the new homeowners were in their twenties and early thirties, young professionals enticed by the low-interest rate loan program and by the chance to be part of an innovative community. The special rate came with the requirement that the owner occupy the property, which ensured that the neighborhood gained truly invested residents. Among the "homesteaders" were employees of the NC National Bank and the *Charlotte Observer*, as well as several independent business owners. The area attracted architects and designers, young families and gay neighbors. All of them had the ability to see the possibilities in the old houses and the new community.

> *The requirement of living in the house made it so that people wouldn't just come in and buy up a house and then flip it. That would just defeat the whole purpose. You had to stay, and then you were part of everything and you wanted to stay.*
>
> —*Rob Carpenter*

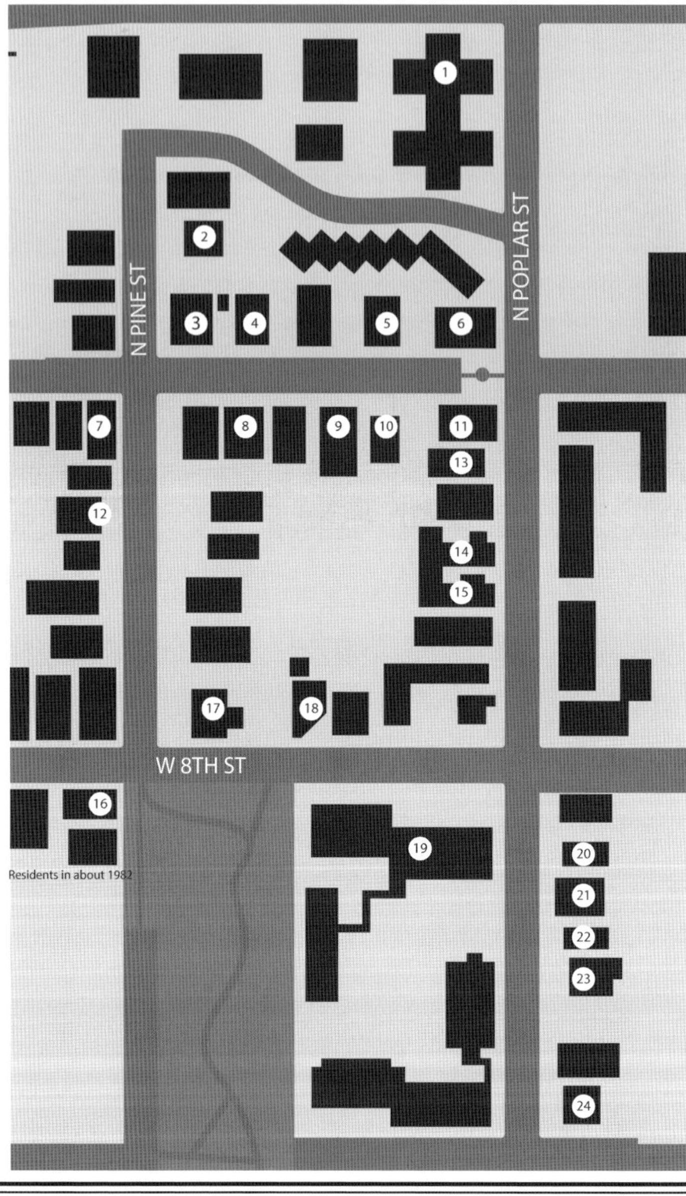

1. Poplar Apartments
2. Betty
3. Hester (The Berryhill House)
4. Rash
5. Tarleton
6. Neal (The Sheppard House)
7. Alexander Michael's
8. Fenimore
9. Romine
10. Smith
11. Bowden-Seymour (The Blair House)
12. Lowry
13. Badger
14. Gantt
15. Watt
16. Rennegar-Coltharp
17. Hefner-Carpenter (The Overcarsh House)
18. Cochran
19. Salvation Army Housing
20. Peters-Nagy
21. Dalton
22. Rankin
23. Taylor
24. Trent

Families and their homes during the renovation of Fourth Ward. *Map by Gau Gupta, modified by the author.*

The Overcarsh House is seen here in the early stage of its stabilization. The surrounding streets are still open and full of traffic; beams stick through windows. The inspector Calvin Hefner hired when he purchased the house discovered numerous problems, the most serious being that the sewer line from an upstairs bathroom had never been connected to the sewer line; it just ran into the basement and emptied at a nearby storm drain. *Courtesy of Catherine Barnhardt Browning.*

Calvin Hefner bought and began restoring the Overcarsh House, at the corner of West Eighth and North Pine Streets. Rob Carpenter soon joined him, and the couple became a mainstay of the neighborhood's social scene and spirit.

The Overcarsh House's exuberant character was soon enhanced with a bright pink paint scheme and fanciful decoration for every holiday. The neighborhood kids especially loved the way that the turret would be lit each December to appear from the street as one gigantic Christmas tree, reaching from the first floor to the roof.

> *My parents thought we were crazy—but we were sort of like "Why not?" It was a great deal, and it wasn't risky in terms of the money because we didn't pay a lot for the house. Nobody came down here and said that they were going to hire somebody to do all the work—but for a lot of us, it was like, we'll live in these two rooms while we redo those two and then we'll move over and keep going.*
>
> —*Gail Fenimore*

Left: The Overcarsh House soon after purchase by Calvin Hefner. *Courtesy of Dennis Rash.*

Below: Overcarsh House looking really beautiful in 1979. *Courtesy of Jim Renegar and Gloria Coltharp.*

The Overcarsh House side view. *Courtesy of Dennis Rash.*

These bungalows on Ninth Street had been by-the-room rentals or sat empty for years before they became the Romine and Fenimore family homes. *Courtesy of Catherine Barnhardt Browning.*

The Rash House seen from the rear, newly placed on its site with no foundation yet. The beams used to move the house are still in place, and one can see where the foundation was opened up to allow the steel beams to be inserted. *Courtesy of Dennis Rash.*

After the houses were relocated, the long process of renovation began. Some homes were in relatively good condition, requiring only cleaning and repainting; others required major construction.

> *We ran out of money pretty quick. And we went through so many contractors! They just didn't know how to work on an old house or didn't want to work in the neighborhood.*
>
> *We ended up doing probably 90 percent of the work ourselves—and there was so much work! I spent hours, weeks it seemed, on those stairs, stripping and sanding and finishing them—the steps, the banisters, the newel posts.*
>
> *—Marsha Rash Sherry*

The Rash House, shown soon after relocation to Ninth Street, needed new stairs and landscaping support in addition to the foundation. It also needed a lot of old woodwork replaced and a new chimney.

The term *sweat equity* gains new meaning when one realizes how much hard physical labor the residents put into their homes. When talking about the houses, many interviewees showed off scars from long-ago mishaps.

The Rash House is shown soon after relocation, with the exterior scraped for painting and boasting a new set of front stairs with a fanciful, curved entrance wall. *Courtesy of Dennis Rash.*

The Rash House with a garbage chute to a trailer and a hole in the roof for the new chimney. *Courtesy of Dennis Rash.*

The Rash House new site without the steps yet. *Courtesy of Dennis Rash.*

Dennis Rash on the porch of his home. *Courtesy of Catherine Barnhardt Browning.*

We looked at a lot of different houses, and they were all just completely dilapidated. We bought the one that we ended up moving for $100, and then the cost of the move was obviously a lot more than that. And a lot of the renovations people did themselves, we did ourselves.

I remember being in the house and pulling the wainscoting off. I was pulling on some, and Dad was pulling it back, and he let go by accident and my hand was in between, and my hand got nailed to the wall. But everybody had stories like that. That happened everywhere; everybody had stories like that.

—*Mebane Rash*

Everyone always had some project or another underway. And we did so much of the work ourselves; we didn't really hire contractors for most of the jobs. Partly because we didn't have the money, but also because we all wanted to do it ourselves—have that ownership—the houses were ours in a different way because we had so much sweat in them. Not just sweat equity—actual blood and sweat.

—*Gail Fenimore*

We really took seriously the part of the agreement that said we were to restore the house, not renovate it. We wanted everything to be perfect, and we probably put in better fixtures and hardware than the house had to begin with! I spent so much time with the fellow who sourced things for us that Gordon started worrying that we were having an affair. But then the bills started rolling in, and he said it would have been cheaper if I was fooling around with him! We replaced the door handles and the light fixtures…even the light switches were antiques that we found.

We found a clawfoot tub that I fell in love with for the upstairs bathroom. This thing was huge, and it was enameled cast iron. I can't even guess how much it weighed. Well, when it was delivered, they put it on the back porch because we were still working on the bathroom. When we got ready to move it, we realized that it was too heavy for just Gordon and [our son] *Bruce to handle. We had to get all of the guys from the neighborhood to wrangle this beast up the stairs. We were paying back those favors for months….*

—*Bev Lowry*

The Lowrys' son Bruce was still in high school when they were in the heaviest work of renovation, taking down the original plaster walls that were too badly damaged to salvage. He and a few friends agreed to work in the house over the summer in exchange for a bit of money plus lunch each day. Their son John recalled that it was especially dirty work because the plaster covered lathing and horsehair insulation, which had captured dust from the coal-burning fireplaces over the decades.

Bruce and his buddies would be just filthy from that coal dust, then they'd go over to a little fried chicken joint up the road and get lunch. At the end of the summer, my dad figured it probably would have been cheaper to hire a construction crew because those boys ate so much chicken!

Dad also stopped by the shop one day and asked the folks there what they thought of those boys who came in every day covered in coal dust. And they said, "We just figured there must be a mine somewhere nearby!"

—*John Lowry*

Creativity and perseverance were the best assets of the neighbors.

When I started on the house on Tenth Street, it didn't have a proper Certificate of Occupancy. I didn't want to keep paying rent on the apartment

Beverly, Gordon and Bruce Lowry working on restoring their home. *Courtesy of Mebane Rash.*

> *I'd had, so I moved in anyway, but it didn't have running water! It wasn't a big deal; I just went to the country club every morning and showered over there, then I'd come back and walk to work. I think I did that for about six months.*
>
> —*Loy McKeithen*

While showering offsite was a challenge, renovating with kids underfoot could be even more difficult. But there were times that they came in handy.

> *The city thought we were nuts. I will never forget, we could not get any permits, we couldn't get anything done. At one point, I was so over it, I said, okay, I'm going to solve this problem. I had a two-year-old and a four-year-old, and I'm going downtown with my children. So I went down to the planning department and I had the kids, and I said, "I really do need to have this appointment so that we can start the work and I would really like some help here."*

And the people there said blah-blah-blah, no help at all. I said nothing; I just waited. But I also didn't say no to anything that the children wanted to do—it was stunning! I had never let them be that bad! They were crawling all over; they were under things and grabbing things and in the way. They totally wiped out that department.

—Nancy Betty

They were your secret weapon!

—Tyson Betty

Suffice to say that she got the permits and was able to move forward with the renovations.

Jim Renegar and Gloria Coltharp renovated 427 North Pine Street after buying it from the Berryhill Foundation. Originally a gracious family home, it had been divided up into rental units and had then become a "liquor house" where people would come to buy drinks when they couldn't afford a whole bottle.

When they completed the purchase, the house was not in habitable condition, so they had to take a conventional mortgage. Conventional loan rates were about double those of the CDC loans, but CDC borrowers had to live in the home, so Jim and Gloria needed to move in as soon as possible. They got the house cleaned up enough to be livable and had it re-inspected, then Jim went to their loan officer to get the mortgage converted to the historic district program. But the loan officer said it just didn't look livable to him and denied the application.

That weekend there was a jazz band and dance party at Spirit Square that Jim and Gloria attended. While spinning around the floor, Jim literally bumped into Hugh McColl and his wife, Jane, apologized and moved on. On Monday morning, Jim began thinking about the conundrum of the house occupancy, the loan and his brief encounter with the president of the bank. He decided to visit the loan officer again and said, "I talked to Hugh over the weekend, and I thought I'd come back and ask you again to take a look at this loan." As he noted, that was all true; he just didn't say what they talked about! The loan officer paled a bit, promised to reconsider and approved the change by the end of the week.

The Berryhill House today is a beloved historic landmark and the anchor property for any exploration of Fourth Ward. The double lot and generous garden seem to have always been the gracious setting for this lovely home, but enormous effort went into its creation. *All color photos courtesy of Austin Caine.*

Number 326 West Eighth Street.

Number 315 West Ninth Street.

Number 316 West Ninth Street.

Number 319 West Ninth Street.

Number 320 West Ninth Street.

Number 323 West Ninth Street.

Number 333 West Ninth Street.

Alexander Michael's Pub at 401 West Ninth Street.

Number 504 North Pine Street.

Number 505 North Pine Street.

Above: Number 509 North Pine Street.

Left: Number 513 North Pine Street.

Number 523 North Pine Street.

Number 601 North Pine Street.

Top: Number 605 North Pine Street.

Bottom: Number 607 North Pine Street.

Number 610 North Pine Street.

Number 400 North Poplar Street.

Number 412 North Poplar Street.

Number 416 North Poplar Street.

Above: Number 420 North Poplar Street.

Right: Number 424 North Poplar Street.

Number 428 North Poplar Street.

Number 523 North Poplar Street.

Number 529 North Poplar Street.

Number 511 North Church Street.

Above: Number 314 West Eighth Street.

Left: The Berryhill House at 324 West Ninth Street.

The Berryhill House decorated for Christmas.

The Berryhill House with patrons of the Holiday Home Tour.

427 N. Pine Street December 1979

Number 427 North Pine, one of the Victorian houses still in its original location, is on the corner of Pine and Eighth Streets. This photo (taken at about the time that Jim and Gloria purchased it) shows pile of lumber in the front yard, just post purchase. *Courtesy of Jim Renegar and Gloria Coltharp.*

At one point in the renovation, they were stripping paint from some of the wainscoting at night and an extension cord sparked near the pile of used rags. Jim recalled thinking that it might be easier to rebuild after a fire than to keep going, but Gloria wisely decided to separate the fire hazards and keep at the woodwork.

The Berryhill House became a family home once again when Jim and Eileen Hester moved in with their children, Kathleen and Jimmy. *Courtesy of Catherine Barnhardt Browning.*

The Cochran house was featured in a *Southern Living* article (November 1980) that celebrated the neighborhood revitalization. The home's modern design within the context of the older neighboring buildings, its site on the narrow lot and the passive solar features were all revolutionary for the time.

Down the street at the Berryhill House, the work of making the house into a functioning home continued. The Junior League had gotten the Berryhill stabilized and safe, but new owners Jim and Eileen Hester still had an enormous amount of work ahead.

> *The first winter, we were so cold in the house because it didn't really have any insulation in the walls and the windows were single-pane glass so the wind just came right through. It felt like we were pretty much camping inside the house.*
>
> —*Jim Hester*

Luckily, Jim and Eileen Hester were an engineer and a nurse, respectively. Their skills and personalities were crucial for a neighborhood full of amateurs with power tools.

> *I'd get a call pretty often from one of the neighbors asking me to come around and look at something they wanted to do. I had to tell folks that they couldn't take out a loadbearing wall or do some crazy thing with wiring. They would want to have it look a certain way, and these houses wouldn't always want to go in that direction.*
>
> —*Jim Hester*

Sometimes, the Hesters were the ones who needed help from the neighbors, as when they were renovating some bathrooms.

> *The two upstairs bathrooms both had old 1950s-style bathtubs, both stained and chipped so badly, they couldn't really be repaired. Eileen said they had to go, so they were going to go. The challenge was that they were heavy as all get out, and they were on the second floor.*
>
> *Well, I got a few of the fellows and we got the smaller one out of the bathroom, but I was worried about getting it down the stairs. I thought that somebody was going to go right over the banister and then get crushed by the damn thing…*
>
> *So we started looking at what we could do, and I realized that the window in the bedroom on the Pine Street side was big enough for the tub to go through and it was a pretty low sill. We looked at it from the outside and saw that that one window wasn't over the porch. There was a straight drop to the yard because the porch stopped about five feet in front of it. So we just dragged the bathtub into that room and levered it up on boards and pushed it out the window!*
>
> *The first one broke in half, but the second one stayed in one piece. It was so heavy! A buddy of mine who had a farm came and got it a few days later and used it as a trough for his cows for a long, long time.*
>
> —*Jim Hester*

In the block of Poplar Street between Eighth and Seventh, houses were being moved in and built, but the one remaining original building at 412 North Poplar was bought by Fred Hill. In addition to stabilizing the foundation, he made the saltbox construction of the rather plain house much more elegant by adding a porch and balcony facing the street and by clearing the lot of debris.

Above: Number 412 Poplar was unoccupied for many years. *Courtesy of Dennis Rash.*

Left: Fred Hill purchased 412 North Poplar in 1976. He renovated it and added the front porch and Georgian-style front steps. *Courtesy of Fred and Jeanie Taylor.*

Fred Hill lived in the upstairs portion of the house while running an antique shop on the main floor with Ellen Davis.

The Taylors, Fred and Jeanie, purchased it in 1979. While they knew that the house wasn't really "finished," they were surprised one morning to find a raccoon had come in through a hole in the attic and made a nest in a corner of their bedroom. Jeanie's encounter with a large mouse in an upstairs toilet alerted them to the need for modernizing the plumbing. Over the next decade, the roof, pipes and electrical systems were updated. The Taylors also replanted an extensive garden in the plot they purchased next door.

Top: Number 412 North Poplar unoccupied and boarded up prior to purchase by Fred Hill. *Courtesy of Fred and Jeanie Taylor.*

Bottom: Number 412 North Poplar at sale in 1986 to Fred and Jeanie Taylor. *Courtesy of Fred and Jeanie Taylor.*

When Fred Hill sold the Poplar Street house and closed the antique business, Ellen Davis purchased the McNinch House at 511 North Church Street.

Notice the neighboring building's sign for the "Women's Rehabilitation Center" and the general condition of the house and grounds. Davis lived upstairs and painstakingly restored the home, stripping mantels, replastering walls, cleaning and repairing windows. She worked on the house for years, bringing her vision of it into being.

Davis installed a commercial kitchen but originally used it to make sandwiches she sold from a pushcart. Every weekday, she would load the cart and wheel it to the corner of Trade and Tryon Streets at the lunch hour, coming home only when she had sold all her inventory. She later ran the front of the house as a gift shop for several years before opening the McNinch House Restaurant in 1988 as one of Charlotte's first high-end dining spots.

It's a challenge to discern the McNinch House behind the overgrown trees and unkempt garden. The neighboring rehabilitation center was sadly typical of the type of businesses that populated the area. Ellen Davis bought the McNinch House in 1979. She transformed the first floor into a commercial kitchen and restaurant and the upper floors into her private residence. *Courtesy of Catherine Barnhardt Browning.*

The McNinch House tucked between the Frederick Apartment building and a house then used as a rehab center. *Courtesy of Dennis Rash.*

Number 316 West Ninth Street prior to renovation, with the windows still boarded over. *Courtesy of Dennis Rash.*

Number 315 West Ninth with boarded-up windows. *Courtesy of Dennis Rash.*

Newlyweds Tom and Gail Fenimore were excited to join the growing community with the purchase of their home on Ninth Street. Gail had grown up in Oak Ridge, Tennessee, where her father worked at the National Laboratory. She loved the sense she had as a child of everyone being deeply invested in the community's success, and they wanted to find something similar that suited their sensibilities.

> *I used to say that Tom and I were closet hippies. We had a bit of a rebellious streak in us that didn't just want to go along to get along.*
>
> *And when you think about it, the people who moved down here really had that same kind of feeling—they were anticipating something different, they wanted the challenge, not the "same old, same old."*
>
> —*Gail Fenimore*

At the Fenimore House on West Ninth Street, the interior walls were so damaged that the plaster had to be removed and replaced with sheet rock, a job for professionals. When workmen removed the fireplace mantels to repair the walls behind them, Gail and Tom saw the chance to start participating in the renovation.

We have four mantels in the house; we took them all out to the apartment where we were living while the house was being worked on. We had them on the balcony, and we stripped them all by hand out there on the patio. And then we brought them back and had them installed back in the house.

We realized one weekend that the workers had scaffolding up from putting up all the sheetrock on the vaulted ceiling and they were almost done. But the ceiling wasn't painted, and they were going to take down the scaffolding when they finished. We ran around and found the only paint store open (I think it was a Sunday) and spent the rest of the day painting before they took away that scaffolding!

—*Gail Fenimore*

The Blair House on the corner of West Ninth and North Poplar Streets was home to Jack Bowden and his partner, David Seymour. Jack often said that his favorite part of the house was the front porch and even installed a phone line there so he could have a little office outside. He could participate in all the gossip and watch the world go by.

Numbers 523 and 529 North Poplar before rehabilitation and infill. The lot between the houses, formerly the garden of the Blair family at 529, was sold for a new home to be built there by architect Michael Finch. The small white flowers seen in the gardens still appear every year.

They later offered the house as Charlotte's first bed-and-breakfast inn and catered numerous weddings and other celebrations.

The Lowry house on the block of Pine Street between Eighth and Ninth presented a unique challenge due to the damage it sustained when it was moved. Because much of the budget for renovation had to instead go toward rebuilding the kitchen, the family took on many tasks themselves.

> *It seemed that every weekend was spent working on the house. There was always some project that Beverly had lined up for us to do, so we'd spend the whole weekend on it. It wasn't like I ever got a break from working on something! And it would almost never turn out quite the way you thought it should look.*
>
> *The thing was, on Sunday afternoon, you'd finally take a shower and pour a drink and go walk around the neighborhood to see what everybody else had been working on. And by the time you'd gotten around and seen how rough their projects were, our house didn't look too bad!*
>
> —*Gordon Lowry*

With so many individual families working on their houses, a strong sense of camaraderie developed. Many residents talked about helping each other with projects and lending equipment or expertise.

> *We all helped each other with projects. And we'd all borrow tools from each other because I would need a sander that you had, and you'd need the table saw that I had. So we had a sort of lending library of power tools because nobody could afford to buy all of it.*
>
> —*Dennis Rash*

CHANGING CHARACTER OF THE COMMUNITY

The renovations, house moves and new construction were making massive changes to an area of Charlotte that had been mostly ignored for decades. When the families that had owned the grand houses moved out to the suburbs over the prior decades, the structures were often sold to nonresident landlords and rented out by the room. Sites of houses that were burned down or demolished became de facto camping grounds.

The streetscapes had taken on an industrial feel, with highway exits running directly into the neighborhood streets, few stop signs, pitted concrete sidewalks and harsh fluorescent lighting.

> *We were the second family to move in, and the Hesters came pretty soon after. And then a lot of people came in the year or so after that. But for a little while, it was a pretty lonely walk home after work. You didn't see anybody coming in this direction at all. The town closed up.*
>
> —*Tom Fenimore*

The approximately 1,600 residents of Fourth Ward in the early 1970s were, frankly, poor people who didn't have other options. George Dunlap was a rookie policeman assigned to walk Fourth Ward in 1976. He recalled few resident owners at the time and great skepticism that the newcomers would be able to change the community as much as they hoped. The people he saw living there were mostly transients who had been pushed out of other places and into Fourth Ward because there weren't many other options in the city. The abandoned blocks of this part of the center city were close to the railroad tracks, the soup kitchen, the highways and the cheap motels along North Tryon Street. There were old mill houses on Pine Street that had been rented out until the City of Charlotte Code Enforcement condemned them; they were boarded up for more than a year awaiting repair. The empty lots and buildings had become the transients' territory, and many of them were not eager to be moved yet again.

Number 424 North Pine Street was a mill house that had been rented out until the City of Charlotte Code Enforcement department condemned it. Here it is shown boarded up, awaiting repair. *Courtesy of Catherine Barnhardt Browning.*

There were also two subsidized apartment complexes housing mostly elderly, indigent people. Edwin Towers (Charlotte Housing Authority, 1967) is on the block bordered by Poplar, Church, Ninth and Tenth Streets. Booth Gardens (the Salvation Army, 1972) is at the corner of Poplar and Seventh Streets.

There were two liquor stores on Graham Street and another one on Church Street; there were no grocery stores, no shops, no restaurants.

> *Literally 50 percent of the parcels were vacant, and what was here was in bad shape.…Many people living in the houses were extremely transient and had lived in Fourth Ward for less than two or three years.*
>
> —*Dennis Rash**

The general approach of the Friends of Fourth Ward was to support economic diversity among the residents while shutting down the illegal trades. While there were certainly people who felt pushed out of the neighborhood, the new neighbors were intentional about limiting collateral damage when possible. The Friends lobbied for the enhanced upkeep and programming at the subsidized housing in the area and included representatives of these residents in neighborhood planning meetings and social events.

Gloria Coltharp was a key connector for some of this work. She and her husband, Jim Renegar, bought 427 North Pine Street, but she came to

* *Charlotte Observer*, January 29, 1978, 5E.

While much of the news coverage of the Fourth Ward was positive, editorial cartoons like this one skewered the optimism of the newcomers. *Courtesy of Jim Renegar and Gloria Coltharp.*

know Fourth Ward initially as a social worker, assisting people seeking help with their housing, health or other needs. She described some of the places people were living in as infested with vermin, dangerous and unsanitary. For example, the Overcarsh House had been divided into six separate rental units. When it was inspected prior to sale, the plumber discovered that the outflow line from an upstairs bathroom had never been connected to the sewage system; it just emptied into the basement drain. As houses were sold for renovation, Gloria often helped residents get out of bad housing into public options in the area.

The determination of the new residents to "clean up" the area encompassed both physical and use of space changes.

The Friends of Fourth Ward lobbied for changes to the streetscape as residents began to cluster around the blocks in the center of the neighborhood.

Television news also took note of the house relocations and other changes to Fourth Ward. The poor street condition of the street and peeling paint on the Sheppard House made a sharp contrast to the optimism of the neighborhood boosters. The film crew is standing near the corner of Ninth and Poplar Streets, an intersection that was blocked by a small park as part of the effort to make the neighborhood more pedestrian oriented. *Courtesy of Dennis Rash.*

In addition to Fourth Ward Park, they petitioned the city for better lighting and sidewalks and for street changes to prioritize walkers over auto traffic. The installation of fountains and small parks at the intersection of Poplar and Ninth and at Pine and Eighth Streets helped to break up the traffic grid and calm the flow of cars and trucks through the neighborhood. The street closures made criminal activity more cumbersome and calmed the speeding traffic through the neighborhood. Changing a few other streets to one-way further reduced through traffic and improved safety. The nearby image of the home at 427 North Pine shows the proximity to the corner of two busy, narrow streets.

These changes would set the tone for the feeling of the neighborhood, but the officials were used to operating without so much resident input and resistant to the changes. Streetlights became a huge issue in the redesign of the street scape.

> *Duke Energy and the city wanted to put in the standard, mercury vapor, industrial lights, and it just was so wrong for the neighborhood because it*

Originally a gracious family home, this house was divided up into rental units and then became a "liquor house" where people would come to buy drinks when they couldn't afford a whole bottle. *Courtesy of Catherine Barnhardt Browning.*

> *was always meant to be pedestrian oriented. The people who understood that would explain that the lights needed to be lower, closer to the people walking on the sidewalk, they needed to be all on the same side of the street, they should be a little bit higher at the intersection so that those were clear… stuff that makes sense when you see it, but Duke Energy had never done that sort of thing and they kept fussing about the cost.*
>
> *The consultant from Boston said that we had to understand how much income this neighborhood was going to generate. Everybody here in Charlotte was worried about the cost of various things, and he just said, "The cost of these streetlights is like pissin' in a lake! Get to it!"*
>
> —*Gail Fenimore*

Social changes proved to be more difficult to effect than the street and sidewalk modifications. There were deep patterns in the neighborhood of drug dealing, violence and especially prostitution.

Rebuilding Fourth Ward, city workers lay a new sidewalk past the historic Overcarsh House (1880).

Charlotte Observer

Workmen laying the brick sidewalks next to the Overcarsh House. *Courtesy of Jim Renegar and Gloria Coltharp.*

Dunlap, the young policeman, said that both the source of and the solution to many of these social problems in Fourth Ward was the couple at 601 North Poplar Street, Babe and Robert Neal.

Mrs. Neal purchased the Sheppard House in 1961 from the estate of the original owner, Dr. John Sheppard. Sheppard built the house for his wife, daughter and three sons and ran a successful pharmacy in Charlotte. All three of the boys died in childhood. His daughter, Edith, married, moved to New Jersey and had three sons of her own. When Mrs. Sheppard died (in about 1950), Dr. Sheppard asked his daughter to move back to Charlotte with her family, offering to give her the house in return. The house was too big for him alone, and he missed the bustle of young life filling it with noise and activity. Edith Sheppard Shaw lived at the house until the late 1950s. As her sons went off to college and the neighborhood declined, she became uncomfortable in the house. She moved to Myers Park in the late 1950s and sold to Babe Neal after her father died. Edith's son Robert Shaw lamented in an interview that the grand chandeliers certainly would have been removed from the house if his mother had known what kind of establishment it would become.*

Mrs. Neal was widely known to be a madam and entertained clients from house. She restyled the Sheppard House décor with extensive use of red velvet on the walls and ceilings as well as much of the furniture. Pat Locke Williamson lived for a time in the Poplar Building in an apartment that

* Interview with Robert Shaw, November 2019.

overlooked the Sheppard House. She said that if there wasn't anything to watch on television, she would take up her binoculars and peek over to the house because there was always some activity there!

During the 1960s, Mr. Neal purchased several properties in the neighborhood that were also used as working houses for the prostitutes who worked for Babe. At the Sheppard House, the Neals erected a six-foot-high electric fence around the property, reportedly because of the amount of cash that the business generated.

Even while they were bringing unsavory trade to the neighborhood, Babe and Robert Neal maintained 601 North Poplar as their residence, and they kept the house in good condition during the years that the rest of Fourth Ward declined.

The Neals were also good neighbors, engaging with the newcomers by distributing poinsettias to neighbors at Christmastime and giving out huge candy bars at Halloween. Tyson Betty's home was across Pine Street from one of the Neals' rental properties, and he described their approach to resolving problems.

> *Robert Neal had moved the ladies of ill repute to another location, and he had rented the house to a transient family. They were not there too long. In the middle of one night, the man was roaring drunk and went out on the front porch and shot off a shotgun into the air. We complained to Robert about it, and the next day, they were gone, just gone. He understood how to protect his interest in the changes that were happening too. Didn't always use the same methods, but….*
>
> *Another time he was driving around in that car—he had a big convertible Rolls-Royce—and stopped to talk and had his hat on the seat next to him. There was someone causing a bit of problem, and we were talking about what to do. He told us not to worry, but we kept talking about it. Then, he just lifted up the hat, and underneath it was a gun! And he just put the hat back down, and that was that.*
>
> —*Tyson Betty*

The Neals gradually sold off the properties that they owned in the Fourth Ward, including, finally, the Sheppard House in 1991.

The problem of prostitution, both on the street and in several of the houses, was not limited to the Neals' house. The police department committed to using undercover agents to try to address the issue, but this did not always go according to plan:

> *Right when we first moved down there, there was still a lot of prostitution around. We watched through the windows, and we learned a lot....*
>
> *One night, there was this one woman who was up at the top of Ninth Street, not doing much, just kind of there. And Mom and Dad had noticed her, and they decided that they were going to ask her to move right along. So they walked up to her and said, "Listen, we're trying to build a family neighborhood. Could you please take your business just a few blocks along east or west?" And she whipped out her badge and said, "I got this!"*
>
> *They kind of walked back to the house with their tails between their legs....*
>
> *—Mebane Rash*

Other homeowners had to run interference between the "working girls" and the workmen who were on their construction sites:

> *When we were under construction on the house and just barely had steps into the front, my guys were upstairs working on the porch roof and I was working again with some of those gallons of paint stripper. I looked out of the back door, and there were women going up the ladder and propositioning my workmen!*
>
> *I went out and shook my paint stripper brush at them and said, "Get down! Go back across the street! You are not allowed over here, and they are not going to work with you!" The women kind of slunk away, and the workmen just said, "Thank you, ma'am," and looked really sheepish.*
>
> *—Nancy Betty*

Even as renovations were completed and new residents moved in, the area struggled to shed its seedy reputation. An example happened at the house that the Lowry family had purchased on Pine Street. They used the first floor as office space for Gordon's company and renovated the second floor as an apartment that they rented to the office manager, a young single woman.

One morning, she was awakened by someone banging on the front door. A "gentleman" had mistaken the directions he had been given to one of the still-active houses of prostitution; he had turned three doors right instead of left on Pine Street. She answered the door and asked, "Can I help you?"

The fellow looked her up and down and answered enthusiastically, "I bet you can!" Understandably, she slammed the door on him and moved out shortly after.

Rob Carpenter remembered recurring problems with the people who were camping in the lot across from his home at the corner of Pine and Eighth Streets. It took months for the campers to understand that the new residents were determined to change the neighborhood.

> *The empty lot was bad. The druggies would set up there and would burn tires and garbage. They'd be doing drug deals. We'd call the cops and call again, and eventually they realized we weren't going to stop. Then things started filling in the empty lots, and the problem people moved out.*
>
> —*Rob Carpenter*

Another incident happened when Jim Renegar arrived home one evening and was greeted by a vagrant who tried to rob him. The man brandished a knife and demanded ten dollars. Thinking quickly, Jim responded that, while he didn't have ten dollars, he did have five, and he told the would-be robber that the knife was just the type of thing he needed and had been looking to buy. Would the "gentleman" sell it to him for the five dollars? The transaction was completed, and that particular fellow did not bother them again.

Homeowners generally described being aware that they were the new element in the mix and that changes would not come overnight. They described taking a "live and let live" approach to most issues even as they were aware of potential conflicts. Sometimes, because the houses are all so close together, neighbors were affected by dramas playing out in the adjacent properties.

> *When we moved in, the house next door* [corner of Ninth and Pine] *was a rooming house. We were using the room closest to that house as a guest room because the upstairs wasn't finished. One weekend we had a friend staying, and in the middle of the night he comes running out of the room saying, "There's gunshots right outside!"*
>
> *Someone* [next door] *had shot into the floorboards during an argument. "Well," we said, "that doesn't usually happen…"*
>
> *—Tom Fenimore*

Susan Cody recalled one incident that had a less happy ending. When leaving the Poplar Building one morning for work, she came upon a neighbor who owned a landscaping business trying to extricate his truck from the scene of a fight from the night before. Two vagrants had gotten into a brawl over a drug deal gone wrong, and one of them grabbed a shovel from the truck and struck the other. Both of the men were discovered the next morning, one passed out and the other deceased.

The change at the Berryhill Grocery Store on the corner of Ninth and Pine was emblematic of the area's transformation. The building had gone through many uses, from grocery store to laundromat to boxing gym; by 1970, it had long been boarded up and used for storage. Cat Belk and Ruth Dalton, two of the Junior Leaguers who had worked on the Berryhill House across the street, purchased the grocery and the adjacent small mill houses. They rented the houses out to new residents and later sold the grocery to Cullie and Sylvia Tarleton, who lived with their family on Ninth Street.

In 1983, the Tarletons sold the site to Michael Troiano and Alexander Copeland. They turned it into Alexander Michael's, a café and grocery

The Berryhill Grocery Store after years of neglect (about 1976). *Courtesy of Jim Renegar and Gloria Coltharp.*

The Berryhill Grocery Store in the early stage of stabilization (about 1977). *Courtesy of Jim Renegar and Gloria Coltharp.*

Steve Casner behind the bar at Alexander Michael's in about 1980. *Courtesy of Steve Casner.*

store, and hired Steve Casner to manage the business. The neighborhood kids loved the reach-in freezer full of ice cream bars, and the "baby bankers" from the office buildings found it a convenient spot for lunch away from the office. By 1983, the business had evolved into a full restaurant and bar.

Casner remembered striving to make the bar a place where everyone felt comfortable and no one group took over. In fact, when some of the fellows from the banks started crowding out the neighborhood regulars, he simply lowered the stock he kept of their preferred beers and liquor—and raised the prices a bit.

In most ways, the demographic, racial and socioeconomic mixture of residents in the neighborhood was seen as a novel and positive attribute. The changes in the social and cultural landscape opened up opportunities for these new neighbors to really get to know people who were, in some ways, very different from themselves. Indeed, many residents came to Fourth Ward seeking that diversity.

There was such a range of people. There were the bankers, of course, and the people like us (gay couple, design background), and some lawyers, but there was also our mailman! The mailman lived over on Eighth Street for years. The mix of people was so unusual, and we all got along because it was A to Z! And when it was time for a party, of course we were all great friends.

—Rob Carpenter

THE CITY GROWS AROUND THE NEIGHBORHOOD

As homeowners worked on their houses and the Community Development Corporation began to create new housing options in the neighborhood, the surrounding city changed too.

> *What we did for you in Fourth Ward was that we built a city around it for you!*
>
> —*Hugh McColl*

Charlotte's civic and business leaders wanted to create the amenities that they found important in other thriving urban centers. They also recognized that growing suburbanization threatened the health of the urban core as early as the 1960s. The Downtown Charlotte Association, a group of business leaders, hired consultants and commissioned architects Odell and Associates to develop a comprehensive plan for remaking the heart of the city. AG "Goolie" Odell led the creation of what came to be called the Odell Master Plan for Charlotte, which was adopted by city council in 1966. In 1975–76, Odell and his team offered up a new iteration of the plan that included a deeper evaluation of cultural assets, existing and needed.

The plan called for theaters and rehearsal space for performing artists, museums for both fine art and children's education and sports facilities for professional teams. The overarching goal was to create a variety of high-quality spaces for civic life. The Odell Master Plan for Cultural Assets identified parts of Charlotte's Uptown (including Fourth Ward) that were best suited to development or adaptive reuse for these purposes.

A Spirit Square street party with mime and jazz band. *Courtesy of John Goyette.*

Spirit Square was the first of the cultural assets to be developed and became the calling card for other projects.

The First Baptist Church building on Tryon Street had been empty since 1972, when the congregation relocated to Second Ward. When Mecklenburg County purchased the building in 1975, it planned to raze the building and create parking for the main library next door. When those plans were announced, local preservationists raised their objections to destroying such a beautiful building on one of Charlotte's main streets for another parking lot, and soon after, the building was identified as a major asset for the city in Odell's Master Plan and saved from demolition.

A group including Bill Williamson (a stockbroker) and Tom Storrs (CEO of North Carolina National Bank at the time) came together to create a plan to renovate the sanctuary as a theater and the remainder of the building as arts flex space, including dance rehearsal rooms, galleries, artist studios and administrative office space.

> *The First Baptist Church had the building on the market for years at that point, and it was not in good condition. There were some homeless people in there, and it had been vandalized some.*
>
> *We raised money to bring in the architect to make the plan for the renovation. That temporary committee became the nucleus of the board.*

It became a true arts center because nobody wanted to come Uptown for just one thing. We knew we couldn't raise the money on just one issue, so we got together with the people who were working on the science museum and created the Children's Bond Campaign. The city was in a terrible depression—real estate was really awful, and people just were really down on Charlotte.

Tom Storrs (at Bank of America) understood that there needed to be an investment in the city, that the bonds would be a stimulative for the whole economy. His selling point for the bonds was that the property value was going down all the time, and the city was concerned that they would end up having to raise the tax basis in Eastover to keep paying for the declining properties in Uptown.

—Bill Williamson, founding board member, Spirit Square

The committee proposed a collection of bonds that they called the Children's Bond Campaign to fund renovation and expansion of the church as Spirit Square, creation of Discovery Place (formerly the Children's Nature Museum) and expansion of the library's educational offerings. The bond referendum passed by a narrow margin and raised $10 million for the package of projects.

In 1976 and 1977, the stabilization of the sanctuary space and rehab of the adjacent offices began. In 1978, a second round of fundraising paid for the start of installation of the theater infrastructure and amenities, and John Goyette was hired as the executive director.

The name Spirit Square grew from the commitment to use the historic church as a meeting place for artists and audiences, students and teachers. Although Bill Williamson said that the real reason was that there were so many drunks hanging around! There were also some really "spirited" conversations about how we could pay for it all.

—John Goyette

Goyette had previously run a variety of small arts organizations in New England and was excited to work with a diverse group of artists in a growing city. The new buildings contained studio space for visual artists, rehearsal space for dancers and galleries for displaying work created on-site. He had experience with creating programs, but the renovations of a historic building presented novel challenges.

> *All the stained-glass windows were removed and sent to a restoration shop on Mecklenburg Avenue. I went over one time to see them, and I didn't ever go back again because it scared me so! They had disassembled every piece of the stained glass and had that on a drawing table. Each one was numbered, and they had a template, but each one had to be re-leaded—every single one of them! It was like the most elaborate jigsaw puzzle you'd see in your life. These were little old guys with pince-nez glasses sitting there, working away on every single piece.*
>
> —*John Goyette*

Part of Goyette's approach to developing the program for the theater was to mix local performers with nationally known artists. He also recognized the importance of programming that appealed to a variety of demographic groups to help develop the habit of coming to the theater. By mixing the types of arts on-site, creation and performance spaces and the ages and interests of the audiences, Spirit Square became the cultural asset that the Odell Plan envisioned.

The theater opened on April 15, 1980, with a street party, and that evening, Joel Grey performed and there was a black-tie opening ceremony party. The Spirit Square Auxiliary continued to host house parties, many in Fourth Ward, after each major performance.

FAMILY LIFE AND GROWING UP IN FOURTH WARD

Some of the early residents of the new Fourth Ward were families with young kids. The buyers of the Berryhill House, the Hesters, had a boy and a girl, as did the Rashes, who moved a house to the lot next door. More families soon joined, moving houses, renovating existing ones or building new ones. The Tarleton kids were a little older, the Betty girls and the Cochran kids were a little younger and the Fenimores started their family shortly after moving on to Ninth Street.

> *There was a swing that we hung in the hackberry tree that abutted all three yards (Rash, Hester and Betty), and that corner became the center of their world in many ways.*
>
> *We joked that we should just start a commune—buy a property big enough for all of us and build little houses for us each and then a big house with a kitchen….But in a way, that's what we did. The kids were always going in and out of each other's houses, and it was good to know that they were always together.*
>
> *—Gail Fenimore*

> *Eileen Hester was such a wonderful person. She was a nurse and her kids were in elementary school, so I thought she knew everything there was to know about kids! They lived right across the street when there weren't too many of us here, and she would help me whenever I felt a little lost. She was just a great resource when I was trying to figure out anything, whether it was the house or the garden or the kids.*
>
> *—Gail Fenimore*

Children on bikes beside the Overcarsh House in 1980. *Courtesy of* Charlotte Observer.

These kids seem to prefer playing on the girders under the newly moved Rash home to any jungle gym! *Courtesy of Dennis Rash.*

Jim Rash is just the right size to perch on the railing of his new old house at 320 West Ninth Street. *Courtesy of Dennis Rash.*

The unfinished attics and basements of houses under renovation were especially well loved. Mebane Rash mentioned that traces remain of the "fort" she built with her brother Jim and the Betty girls in the attic of the Rash home.

> *And the kids would have projects too. The fortresses, and then Jimmy Hester got tormented a lot. There was a fair amount of mixing concoctions, of like mustard and Worcestershire and sugar, and watching Jimmy drink it to see if he survived. It was very dramatic!*
>
> —*Mebane Rash*

A favorite activity for Kathleen Betty and Jim Rash was to put on plays in the foyer of the Bettys' Pine Street home. They would spend days planning the production and costumes and inviting the neighbors as well as their parents to attend. When the opening day arrived, Mebane Rash would charge admission (even to the Betty parents) and seat the audience. Jim and Kathleen would begin the performance…and start laughing so hard at their own jokes that they couldn't say their lines!

Another frequent activity was playing "school" on the curving steps of 320 West Ninth Street. Sonja Gantt, as one of the older kids, was the teacher and would quiz the younger children, moving them up or down the stairs as their answers merited.

A playground was built for the kids on Ninth Street. The project brought together neighbors and artists from the newly developed program at nearby Spirit Square.

The little park was well loved, though not always for the reasons the planners intended. Blair Fenimore recalled hanging out there as a teenager and bumming cigarettes from some of the vagrants!

The center of the block surrounded by Eighth, Ninth, Pine and Poplar Streets was another playground of sorts for the neighborhood kids. It was undeveloped except for the Gantt-Watt tennis court. The Fenimore and Badger children especially enjoyed exploring the "forest" in their backyard. Sometimes their exploration included the homes: Cindy Gantt recalled waking up one morning to a small noise on the porch off the master bedroom. She and Harvey cautiously slid open the glass door to see Erin

Top: Ninth Street Playground. *Courtesy of Tom and Gail Fenimore.*

Bottom: The mural at the Ninth Street Playground was a community project, giving the children a chance to help make the space their own. *Courtesy of Tom and Gail Fenimore.*

Top: The Ninth Street Playground mural included silhouettes of residents and artists who helped install it. *Courtesy of Tom and Gail Fenimore.*

Bottom: The Ninth Street Playground mural showing playground equipment and silhouettes. *Courtesy of Tom and Gail Fenimore.*

Badger, then about seven years old, peeking in over the railing. She had been early-morning exploring and climbed up the trellis but panicked a little when she realized how high up she was. They pulled her up onto the porch and sent her off to home, safely, through the front door.

And once the intersection with Poplar was closed and turned into a small park, Ninth Street itself became a play space for the whole neighborhood. The block between Poplar and Pine is a slight downhill slope, and it became the standard place for kids to learn to bicycle and roller skate.

The construction work happening around the neighborhood was a source of endless fascination for the children. Sometimes, the workers even contributed supplies, such as when the electrical and telephone wires were being put underground and the contractors left behind the large wooden spools that had held the wiring.

> *So we took out several of the slats and lined the inside with foam and pillows and carpets. We would put each other in the spools and, you know that little round fountain park at the top of Ninth Street? We would roll children down towards Alexander Michael's (then it was a little ice cream shop).*
>
> *And people would stand down there and theoretically ward off traffic, but my brother almost got hit by a car one time, and that caused some drama.*
>
> *—Mebane Rash*

There was a mix of ages from very young to teenagers, but they tended to all go around together because there weren't that many kids to play with. You'd play with someone a bit older or younger because that's who was around.

Younger kids were fascinated by the older ones' activities, teenagers babysat and organized kids' activities at neighborhood gatherings.

One of the young adults, Joe Grier, bridged the age gap as a law school graduate back in Charlotte as a new lawyer. He knew Marsha and Dennis Rash from attending First Presbyterian Church with his family; when they completed the construction of the apartment in the basement of their home, he moved in as their first renter.

> *It was very open and friendly, and everyone knew each other. There weren't very many kids, but they were always around and were fun.*
>
> *I got the idea at some point to put on this rubber* [Halloween] *mask leftover from college, and I had a long black choir robe and I'd pretend to be "the skeleton man" and run around the neighborhood. It wasn't a big thing for me, but the kids would get so tickled about it.*
>
> —*Joe Grier Jr.*

Grier would give the parents a call to both warn them and confirm that they would unlock the doors, but for the children, the appearance was always a big surprise.

> *At night in the summers, Joe would don this costume of a skeleton. He created this "Skeleton Man" experience for all of us kids. Skeleton Man would just show up on summer nights! He would come around and dart in and around of the old houses.*
>
> *It was a thing and it was awesome, and we all loved it.*
>
> —*Mebane Rash*

As the kids got older and the center city amenities were developed, the kids explored and took advantage of their ease of access.

> *We had free reign of the city; we could walk anywhere, and we did! Perspective is relative when you're a kid—it was just our city. We didn't think anything of walking anywhere we wanted to walk.*
>
> *We spent countless hours at the library. Back when you could rent the big movies that were on the reels. Jim and I would walk back carrying these huge reels to watch in the basement of the house when we were renovating it.*
>
> —*Mebane Rash*

For the parents, giving the kids freedom to roam was both good for them and practical. The kids could walk to the library and park, teens could get themselves to their jobs at Ivey's or Belk department stores. The creation of Discovery Place and Spirit Square gave the young families options for after-school activities and summer arts camps.

Dannye and Ben Romine bought a house on Ninth Street to renovate but divorced before it was completed. Dannye moved into an apartment at the Poplar, while Ben moved into the house. It was so much easier than some situations, Dannye said, because the boys could just walk back and forth as

Patrick Romine (*center*) walking to school with Jim and Mebane Rash. *Courtesy of Mebane Rash.*

they wanted to. They didn't have to be driven everywhere, and they grew up knowing how to manage things themselves.

The families also found ways to take advantage of their urban setting to gain some suburban amenities.

> *The motel at the corner of Tryon and Tenth Street had a swimming pool, and we could buy summer passes for the pool. So that was our little swim club!*
>
> *—Gail Fenimore*

The parks, large and small, were also well loved by the families. Fourth Ward Park stretches over parts of the blocks between Poplar and Pine, Sixth and Eighth Streets. Urban cemeteries provide green space as well as opportunities for restful reflection.

> *The green spaces and the trees are so important. We used to go over to* [Elmwood-Pinewood] *cemetery to watch the trains, and one time it started to rain while we were there. So, we ducked under one of those huge*

magnolias. It started to get dark, but we couldn't go home because it was just pouring rain. We just stayed there under that tree for about half an hour, talking and waiting for the rain to stop. The boys still remember that.

—Robin Cochran

There are also small green areas carved out of many of the developments. For example, the large hackberry tree on Settler's Lane was the perfect size for climbing and sturdy enough to support a multitude. Kids could climb up and be almost invisible to the passersby below. The younger ones thought of it as a great place to spy on grownups, and the teenagers sometimes used it for romantic assignations.

BUILDING COMMUNITY

As more owner-residents came to the Fourth Ward, the personality of the community began to take shape. Most of the people who were interested in being part of the community had an open, adventurous approach and were proactively engaged in making their "village." The formal creation of Friends of Fourth Ward and the Holiday Home Tour were supported by the network of friendships among the neighbors.

> *People came here and wanted to be part of something; they didn't move here just to sit inside and watch the world go by.*
>
> —*Rob Carpenter*

The desire for community was a consistent motivation for early residents. One urban settler said that the "secret sauce" in bringing the community together was pretty simple:

> *It wasn't much a secret—it was alcohol! Lots and lots of cheap wine! We enjoyed being together and having parties and just having some fun with the people around us. Everybody was game, and that made a big difference.*
>
> —*Jim Hester*

In 1976, the neighbors decided to form an official organization, Friends of Fourth Ward, to support their growing community. The Friends intentionally included both property owners and renters, residents and nonresidents who were engaged in the neighborhood. This allowed them to be much more active than a typical homeowners association and to have a broad perspective on the needs of the growing and changing community. As noted earlier, the group lobbied the city to install the brick sidewalks, to add street closures and stop signs to slow traffic, and to create a neighborhood-specific parking program.

They supported enforcement of laws against panhandling and public drinking while also supporting the creation of public housing in the neighborhood. They insisted that new streetlights were consistent with the historic character of the streetscape.

Friends of Fourth Ward also built community spirit within the neighborhood by hosting social activities including picnics in the park and an arts festival. Most significantly, they began Holiday Home Tour to promote the neighborhood to a wider Charlotte audience.

The first Holiday Home Tour was held on December 11, 12, 18 and 19 of 1976. It included the Berryhill House and several other homes under

Looking southeast, the construction of a small park at the former intersection of West Ninth and Poplar Streets. Number 529 North Poplar is at right, and the new fire station is in the background. *Courtesy of Cullie and Sylvia Tarleton.*

Above: Ninth Street seen from the site of the new park. The concrete sidewalks and industrial lights would soon be removed. *Courtesy of Cullie and Sylvia Tarleton.*

Left: Ninth Street from the site of the new parks. The light poles are gone, and bricks have been stacked to repave the sidewalks. *Courtesy of Cullie and Sylvia Tarleton.*

renovation or construction. The neighbors hoped to raise some money and to promote the idea of living in the center city.

One remarkable aspect of these early tours was the collaboration between the Friends of Fourth Ward and volunteers from the Berryhill Foundation, the Junior League and the Citizens for Preservation. All of them brought the sense that they were in the work together, whether they were lobbying for zoning, raising money or throwing a tour and party.

> *The home tour at Christmastime started out as a candlelight tour for two reasons, really. First of all, some of the houses didn't have electricity turned on yet! We would run extension cords from one house to another to work with the power tools, but we knew we couldn't light up the houses enough on extension cords.*
>
> *And secondly, in candlelight, all of the things that would look just terrible in the daytime were harder to notice. People could see the charm of the houses and the neighborhood without seeing the lumps and bumps.*
>
> —*Catherine Barnhardt Browning*

The tour got extensive coverage in the *Charlotte Observer*, partly because the neighborhood was still such a novel development. In the early years, houses were still being moved into the area, and there was a vast range in the condition of the houses. The newly placed buildings were often included to interest possible buyers, but residents also decorated and showed off their renovated homes.

> *During the tour, we stayed at the house the whole time. We would greet people, answer questions and talk with everyone. All of us were really proud of our houses because we had worked so hard on them and done so much of the work ourselves.*
>
> —*Rob Carpenter*

The neighbors who didn't open their homes for the tour helped in other ways. The adults sold tickets and served as docents for the houses on tour. There was always abundant entertainment from carolers and street musicians. Kids would set up a hot cider stand, and Jimmy Hester sold "Real Fourth Ward Pine Cones" until his parents caught on.

Within a few years, it had become both a major fundraiser and a major social event for the residents.

This page and opposite: Home Tour carolers. *Courtesy of Tom and Gail Fenimore.*

A brass band plays for the 1978 Holiday Home Tour at the corner of Eighth and Pine Streets. *Courtesy of Jim Renegar and Gloria Coltharp.*

> *David Seymour, who organized the tour for Friends of Fourth Ward, said that the group had expected to sell about 500 tickets. By dusk Sunday night, they had sold more than 800.*
>
> —Charlotte Observer*

Seymour was the original tour manager and lived at 529 North Poplar Street with his partner, Jack Bowden. He set up the tour ticket booth in their garden at the corner of Ninth and Poplar, where it is still set up each year.

> *In the early years somebody was always under construction, so that was where we'd go for a party; it was open and nothing was going to get messed up! The first year we were on the tour, there was no furniture at all in this room* [study in the front room of the house], *so we just got this massive Christmas tree and put it right in the middle of the room!*
>
> *It was a candlelight tour that ended up here. We had nothing in here, so it was a great place for the party! And everyone who had gone touring ended up at the house—neighbors and everybody else.*
>
> —*Gail Fenimore*

The tour proved to be enormously popular with regional visitors as well as with the neighbors themselves. Each year, different houses were shown, and each year, the number of tickets sold rose.

In 1984, the holiday tour had a separate preview party. One week before the tour opened, three of the original restorations held a simultaneous cocktail party. The idea was to entice people to come to the neighborhood twice, bringing more guests for the full walking tour on the second weekend.†

By 2019, the Holiday Home Tour regularly sold more than two thousand tickets each year, and the tour has raised almost half a million dollars in total.

* *Charlotte Observer*, vol. 94, December 11, 1979, 20. NewsBank: America's News—Historical and Current, infoweb.newsbank.com

† Charlotte Observer, November 30, 1984, 2D. Archival clipping.

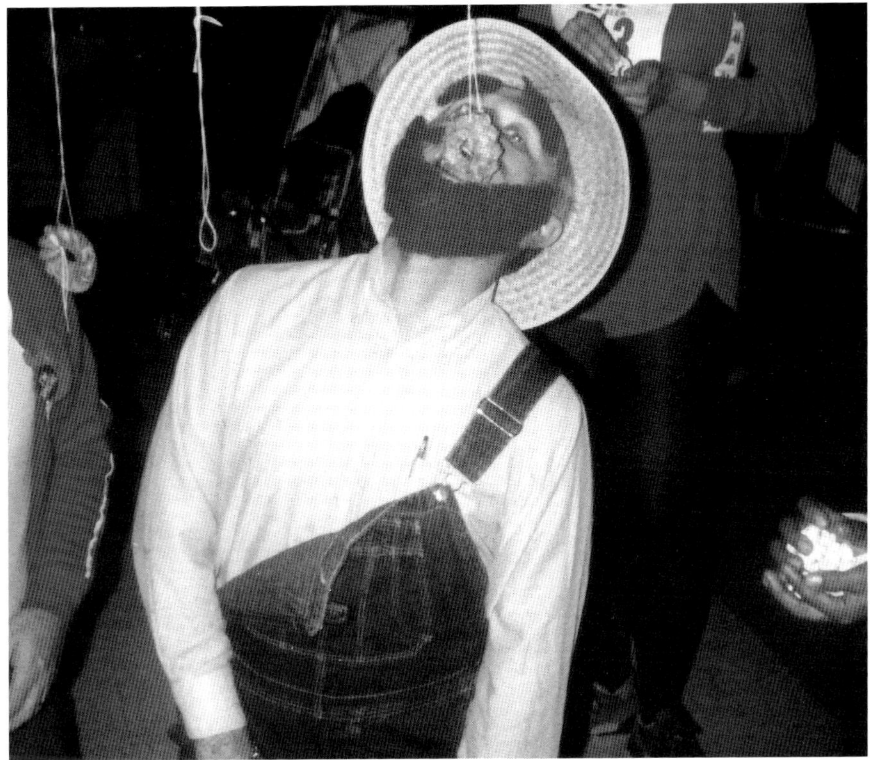

Cullie Tarleton bobbing for donuts at the Fourth Ward Halloween party. *Courtesy of Tom and Gail Fenimore.*

Friends of Fourth Ward uses these proceeds to fund donations to local schools, arts programs and preservation work, as well as to host neighborhood events.

In addition to the tour parties, Halloween activities became a highlight for the neighbors, adults as well as children. Because the area was still filling in and parts were not well lit, the parents organized a neighborhood trick-or-treat in the basement community room at First Methodist Church. The parents came up with a twist on bobbing for apples that would allow costumes and face paint to remain dry: they ran a string through apple donuts and tied them along a broomstick suspended from the ceiling. "Bobbing for donuts" was a hit with both the kids and adults!

> *In just a few years, there were slews of children! We had the Halloween parties at First Methodist basement. They were all ages, and they all played together—it was so good for all of us.*

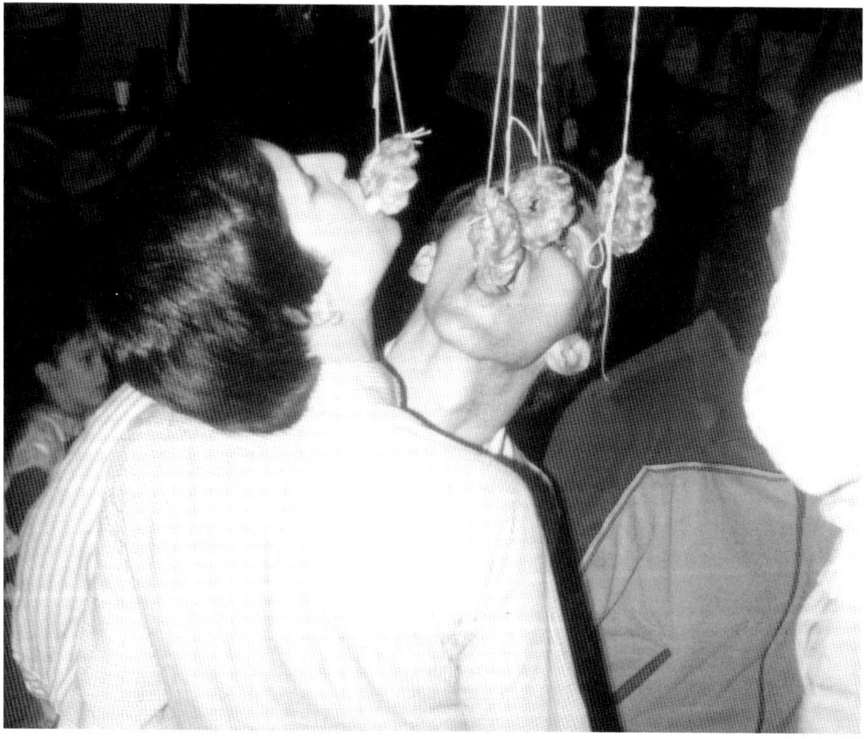

Opposite, top: Erin Badger attacks the Halloween pinata. *Courtesy of Tom and Gail Fenimore.*

Opposite, bottom: Kids bobbing for donuts. *Courtesy of Tom and Gail Fenimore.*

Above: The kids circled up for the costume contest. *Courtesy of Tom and Gail Fenimore.*

> *Halloween was very old fashioned for the kids; we had donut or apple bobbing and games.*
>
> *And then there were some very adult parties that the gay guys would throw. It was always a big thing to have a couples costume or a theme. Tom and I went as a cigarette and a match one year. Calvin was the Fruit of the Loom bunch of grapes, and I think Rob was a banana!*
>
> —*Gail Fenimore*

The adults' Halloween party rotated to various houses in the early years, often landing at whichever site was the most "under construction but still safe" in the neighborhood. Partly because so many of the early residents were gay men who loved drag, it became a tradition for couples to gender-switch for their costumes. Bev Nagy and Jim Peters hosted for years and came up with the idea for another fundraiser for the local firemen. At the annual Drag Ball, contestants for Miss Fourth Ward would collect votes (in the form of contributions), and the winner would be paraded through the neighborhood on the fire truck—lights but no sirens!

Sadly, no photographs of Miss Fourth Ward winners were available for publication.

Another memorable party occurred during a snowstorm in March 1983. Calvin Hefner had contracted to host a party at the Overcarsh House for a group of design professionals attending a conference in Charlotte. Most of the attendees were driving in from out of town, and the event was to be a fancy cocktail party followed by a formal dinner. While snow is not rare in Charlotte, this storm really blew up just days before hitting the region. It became much more severe and changed path, completely closing the roads and airports.

But most of the arrangements for the event were complete before the clients realized that they couldn't get to Charlotte for the party. The house had been decorated, the food had been prepared and, perhaps most importantly, the wine and liquor had been delivered! The client called and told Calvin to just cancel the party and bill them for whatever had already been spent.

Calvin and his partner, Rob, called everyone in the neighborhood to come over and enjoy the party. Every neighbor interviewed for this project remembers the "snow day party," including the children. The grownups arranged sofas, pillows, sleeping bags and blankets in the sitting room with a television playing kids' movies. The adults kept the party going in the rest of the house for the full weekend. Rob recalled that some people went home for a little nap and came back for the next meal.

Most of the children of the Fourth Ward attended neighborhood schools. These schools were integrated both racially and socioeconomically, in part because the surrounding areas were predominantly low income and African American. While the grownups were sometimes wary in their interactions, the children seemed to hardly notice.

Number 424 North Poplar Street in the mid-1980s in the snow. *Courtesy of Fred and Jeanie Taylor.*

One year, Christine's birthday fell on Easter, so I said, of course, we'll have a big Easter egg hunt party that afternoon in Fourth Ward Park. She was at Irwin [Elementary School], *so we invited all of her friends, the whole class, and half of the children were Black and half were white, and they all came in their* [Easter] *outfits. We had hidden eggs for them, and it was such fun.*

When I sent the pictures [to the grandparents], *they were a little surprised, but the kids all had a great time! All dressed up and having a ball.*

—*Nancy Betty*

In addition to the holiday parties, the everyday mix of personalities one encountered kept things lively.

Susan Cody lived at the Poplar Building and would chat with neighbors each morning as she walked to work Uptown. A couple in the condos on Poplar Street were famously flamboyant men, one of whom would water their garden each morning. One morning, he was in a yellow and orange muumuu with a cigarette and coffee cup in one hand and hose in the other, "cussing up a storm" as she passed by. He stopped mid-rant when he saw Susan and said, "Don't mind me honey, I'm just havin' a fit!" She said she never could quite look at him again without thinking of that muumuu.

A favorite neighborhood character was Simmons Jones, scion of the "old Charlotte" Morehead and Dowd families. After serving in World War II, he studied photography in New York, Rome and Paris and worked for *Vogue* magazine and other fashion publications before returning to live in Charlotte.

Simmons Jones—there was only one Simmons Jones! He was born and raised here in Charlotte and then went on to do the fashion work. His family had loads of money, but his brother died in the war, so he had to come back to Charlotte.

We used to have lunch every Friday at Alexander Mike's. He was an absolute stitch and had a great sense of humor, wore a cotton ascot, so smart and so interesting. He'd been everywhere and done everything. Lived alone with his little Pekinese, Dilly.

His apartment at the Poplar was something to see. He painted the whole room with clouds—going from sunrise to sunset.

And he was the one who decided to keep a bar cart in the elevator! He kept it stocked with liquor and glasses, just brought ice. It [the elevator] *broke down so often that he didn't want to be stuck without resources.*

—Rob Carpenter

Another early resident, Gene Humphreys, described the sense of fun and excitement. It was the place where all the interesting guys were, where the interesting parties were. Fourth Ward was the neighborhood you always heard about, so of course, you wanted to go!

There were so many interesting people, and everyone really wanted to be there, to be part of it. We were all thrown into the same mix, so were all part of the same thing, the same family almost. And many people were not close to their original family, so we kind of made our own.

—Rob Carpenter

And the straight (and often rather strait-laced) neighbors were part of the fun, too.

It was the end of a party and getting kind of late, and there were just a few of us hanging around—it was Nancy and Ty [Betty] *and us—and Fred Hill says, "Let's go clubbing!"*

We went to a gay bar out on Wilkinson Boulevard and we went dancing and had the best time, and then all of the sudden, they were closing, so Fred said, "Let's go somewhere else!" We went on to a couple of other places—ended up at four or five in the morning! Then we came back, and Fred cooked breakfast for all of us!

—Tom Fenimore

The neighbors also helped each other through life changes and celebrations. Catherine Barnhardt Browning had gone through a difficult divorce when it was still relatively uncommon. She said that the friendships she had formed with several of the gay couples in Fourth Ward were a crucial support in navigating that phase of her life.

> *I had a daughter get married around that time, and Dennis* [Cudd] *came to my house almost every night. He helped me wallpaper, he planted flowers, he zipped up my dress and drove me to the church. They were such good friends. That spirit of conviviality was such a big part of it.*
>
> *—Catherine Barnhardt Browning*

The parties attracted people from outside of the neighborhood, too. Robin Cochran was a generous and active hostess for both personal events and for Spirit Square.

> *When my parents had their fiftieth anniversary, we gave a big party at the house. Mother was old school, and I said, "We'll have it at the house and have it catered." All of her friends were really curious, and they all came. Mother said, "They'll probably be afraid to come, "but they all showed up! And they all went home carrying on about how nice it was.*
>
> *—Robin Cochran*

The Spirit Square Auxiliary hosted after-performance parties, which were often a mix of musicians, staff, patrons and neighbors. Because the Uptown area had a deficit of restaurants and bars, the post-parties weren't just a nicety. Otherwise, there was nothing for out-of-town visitors or performers to do!

Robin Cochran recalled one performer appreciated the hospitality but didn't enjoy the local "special sauce" as much as the neighbors did.

> *For a while, Spirit Square was the only act in town, but there were things happening there two or three nights a week. We* [the Auxiliary] *would be responsible for entertaining the entertainers after the performance.*

We had Chubby Checker, we had Joel Grey, Jerry Mulligan, Stephan Grapelli [violinist]. *Everybody who came to perform would come back to the house after.*

One of the guys wouldn't drink my wine because we just had big jugs of cheap wine, and he sent somebody out to pick up something else! He said, "I am sorry, I really am…but I just can<u>not</u> drink that wine!"

—*Robin Cochran*

LIFE GOES ON

After the heady days of the early renovation of the neighborhood, the community settled into many of the patterns and routines that happen in every "village." A few couples divorced, though in several cases, both members stayed in the neighborhood. Dennis and Marsha Rash divorced but both stayed in the neighborhood; Dennis later married Betty Chafin and lived in the neighborhood until his death in 2017. Dannye and Ben Romine also divorced, but they lived within a block of each other for the years that their sons were in school.

After her time with the Citizens for Preservation, Patsy Kinsey launched a political career. She served as a Mecklenburg County commissioner from 1990 to 1994 and as a Charlotte City Council member from 2003 until 2017, with a brief interim as Charlotte's mayor.

The low-interest loans that allowed many of the owners to get into the houses eventually led to some having to sell before they really wanted to do so. The loans had a fifteen-year term, and at that point, borrowers had to make a large payment on the loan and refinance any outstanding debt. Many of these loans came due in the midst of the recession of the early 1990s, and several families found they could not meet the financial burden of the houses without the favorable loans.

Jim and Eileen Hester sold the Berryhill House when Jim was laid off and the balloon payment came due, but they lived in nearby Third Ward and were always looking for an opportunity to return. Sadly, Eileen was diagnosed with pancreatic cancer and died in November 1999.

Jack Bowden and David Seymour broke up, and Jack sold the house on Poplar Street. In 1987, he bought the Van Landingham estate on The Plaza, renovating it and running it as an event space until his death from AIDS in 1994.

The kids grew up, and many of them made choices that they trace back to the neighborhood. Sonja Gantt became a journalist and then an advocate for public education. Mebane Rash got a law degree and taught at law school before she, too, became an advocate for public education as CEO of EdNC. Her brother Jim became an Oscar award–winning actor and writer. Jim Hester made a business of renovating old houses in the Atlanta, Georgia area, and Hugh Romine does both old and new construction in Charlotte. Dan Forest became an architect before entering politics and serving as the lieutenant governor of North Carolina. Erin Badger became a dancer and teacher working with special needs students. Gordon and Beverly Lawry's son Bruce had worked with them as they restored the Pine Street house; he was diagnosed with ALS in 1997 and died in early 2001.

The CDC continued redevelopment efforts in other Charlotte neighborhoods, especially in Third Ward and Cherry. In 1996, it was transformed into a nonprofit, Charlotte Center City Partners, and continues to support development and business activities in the area. The development of the surrounding Uptown blocks has continued almost unabated, with apartments and luxury condominiums sharing the skyline with corporate spaces. The population of Fourth Ward in 2023 is approaching four thousand people.

The economic impact of investment in Fourth Ward has exceeded even the most optimistic predictions of the early promoters. In 1983, the Planning Department for the City of Charlotte reported that combined public and private efforts invested $39 million in Fourth Ward between 1975 and 1983. Tax revenues increased to more than 500 percent of their previous level ($583,000 versus $108,000). Similarly, the aggregate value of taxable property in the historic district had risen to $45.5 million, seven times the value of the parcels in 1975.*

Hugh McColl and Harvey Gantt both cite the revitalization of Fourth Ward among their proudest achievements, aside from their respective families.

George Dunlap served as a police officer in the Charlotte-Mecklenburg School System, then was elected to the school board. After fourteen years

* Kathleen Curry, "City Winding Up Fourth Ward Effort, Area Across Graham Gets Aid," *Charlotte Observer*, Decmber 4, 1985, 1.

Holiday Home Tour carolers in 2006. *Courtesy of Jim Renegar and Gloria Coltharp.*

there, he ran for and was elected to the Mecklenburg County Commission in 1998. He became chairman of the commission in 2014 and holds that position still.

After managing the restaurant for twenty-two years, Steve Casner bought Alexander Michael's from Michael Troiano and Alexander Copeland in 2005. He continues to run it today.

Fred and Jeanie Taylor hosted the neighborhood children for the Easter egg hunt each year until about 2006. There were so many new families with young kids that the festivities were moved across the street to Fourth Ward Park. Each year, the teenagers manage the hunt, hiding eggs on the lawn and edges of the landscaping. The local firemen bring the Easter bunny and then spend time with the kids, running sack races and losing tug of war.

The Holiday Home Tour continues as the main source of fundraising for the Friends of Fourth Ward. By 2019, the tour regularly sold more than two thousand tickets each year, and it has raised almost half a million dollars in total. Friends of Fourth Ward uses these proceeds to fund donations to local schools, arts programs and preservation work, as well as to host neighborhood events. There is now a companion Secret

Garden Tour each spring, highlighting the small private spaces residents have created around their homes.

Volunteers still provide hundreds of hours selling tickets, serving as tour guides and caroling to entertain guests to our beloved neighborhood.

WHO'S WHO

Interviewed by Cameron Holtz

Tyson and Nancy Betty
Homeowners at 610 North Pine Street

Catherine Barnhardt Browning
Junior League of Charlotte
Berryhill Foundation

Rob Carpenter
Homeowner at 326 West Eighth Street

Steve Casner
Owner, Alexander Michael's

Robin Cochran
Junior League of Charlotte
Homeowner at 318 West Eighth Street

George Dunlap
Mecklenburg County Commission Chair

Tom and Gail Fenimore
Homeowner at 323 West Ninth Street

Harvey Gantt
Mayor of Charlotte
Homeowner at 517 North Poplar Street

Margaret Bowden Gilleskie
Resident at 529 North Poplar Street

John Goyette
Executive director, Spirit Square

Joe Grier
Resident

Calvin Hefner
Homeowner at 326 West Eighth Street

Jim Hester
Homeowner at 324 West Ninth Street (The Berryhill House)

Kimm Jolly
Berryhill Foundation

Patsy Kinsey
Citizens for Preservation
Charlotte City Council

Gordon and Bev Lowry
Homeowners at 519 North Pine Street

Hugh McColl
Bank of America

Loy McKeithen
Homeowner at 328 West Tenth Street, 324 West Ninth Street

Dan Morrill
UNC Charlotte, Historic Landmarks Commission

Rolfe Neill
Charlotte Observer
Berryhill Foundation

Ed Perzel
UNC Charlotte, Citizens for Preservation

Dennis Rash
Homeowner at 320 West Ninth Street, 610 North Pine Street

Jim Renegar and Gloria Coltharp
Homeowners at 427 North Pine Street

Marsha Rash Sherry
Homeowner at 320 West Ninth Street

Mel Watt
Congressman
Homeowner at 515 North Poplar Street

Bill Williamson
Spirit Square Board of Directors
Homeowner at 510 North Church Street

Pat Locke Williamson
Charlotte City Council
Resident at the Poplar Building

Erin Badger Coffee, Webb Cochran, Blair Fenimore, Keenan Fenimore, Sonja Gantt, Jimmy Hester, John Lowry, Mebane Rash, Brian Watt, Jason Watt
Neighborhood kids

Referenced but Not Interviewed

David Burkhalter
City Manager for the City of Charlotte
Member of First Presbyterian Church

Ellen Davis
Owner of the McNinch House

Joe Martin
Bank of America

RESEARCH NOTES

Charlotte Observer, December 4, 1985.

J. Murrey Atkins Library. "Simmons Jones oral history interview, 1993 February 28." repository.charlotte.edu//islandora/object/uncc:80.

Minutes of City Council meetings, June 7, 1976; July 10, 1978.

ABOUT THE AUTHOR

Cameron Holtz is the former executive director of Historic Charlotte, Inc., and a board member of Friends of Fourth Ward. She has served other history and heritage groups around Charlotte in a variety of capacities, from giving tours and raising money to deciphering handwritten documents and re-installing lost gardens at historic houses. She continues to research, discover, and share connections between the past and present. Cameron shares a historic home in Fourth Ward with her husband and three daughters.